STORYTELLING VOCABULARY STORYTELLING VOCABULARY STORYTELLING VOCABULARY

# 스토리텔링 보카강사 되다!

E-field Academy

그린

MP3 음성파일

Dictation 시험지 제공

We're 위아북스

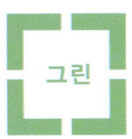

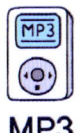

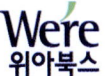

# STORYTELLING VOCABULARY

- 지은이     E-field Academy
- 발행인     조상현
- 발행처     (주) 위아북스
- 주소       서울시 마포구 공덕동 풍림빌딩 304호
- TEL        02-725-9988
- FAX        02-725-9863
- 등록번호   제 300-2007-164호

ISBN  978-89-6614-021-3
www.wearebooks.co.kr

Copyright ⓒ 2013 WEAREBOOKS

이 책의 모든 저작권은 (주)위아북스에 있으므로 일체의 무단 전재 및 모방은 법률로 금지되어 있습니다.
저자와의 협의에 따라 인지는 붙이지 않습니다. 잘못 만들어진 책은 구입하신 곳에서 교환해 드립니다.

STORYTELLING VOCABULARY STORYTELLING VOCABULARY STORYTELLING VOCABULARY

# 스토리텔링 보카강사 되다!

E-field Academy

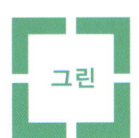

그린

# Introduction

많은 사람들이 영어 단어를 습득하는 것이 영어를 학습하는 데 있어서 기본이 된다는 것을 압니다. 하지만 단순히 단어를 암기하는 것으로는 충분하지 않다는 것을 아는 사람은 많지 않습니다. 한 언어를 익히기 위해서, 학생들은 이러한 단어들을 사용하는 방법과 단어들의 진정한 의미를 배우는데 시간을 소비해야 합니다. 그러나 많은 사람들이 단어를 학습하기보다 여전히 암기하는데 수많은 시간을 소비합니다.

대부분의 단어 책들이 매우 어렵고 지루한 것도 더욱 문제가 됩니다. 다행히도, 단어를 학습하는데 있어서 여러분의 관점과 접근법을 바꿀 방법이 있습니다. 이제 여러분은 재미있는 방식으로 단어실력을 향상할 수 있습니다. 스토리텔링 보카강사 되다! 는 여러분의 어휘력을 확대해 주고 동시에 영어 실력을 향상해줄 것입니다.

이 시리즈는 듣기, 읽기, 쓰기, 그리고 이해력 모두를 다루면서 영어를 학습하는 데 있어서 통합적인 접근법을 사용합니다. 또한, 이 시리즈의 주요한 특징 중 하나는 몇몇 인물들의 일상생활을 둘러싼 내용과 그들이 성장하면서 마주치는 어려움을 포함한다는 것입니다. 각각의 일화를 읽음으로써, 여러분은 영어 단어의 자연스럽고 실용적인 사용법을 배우게 될 것입니다.

이 시리즈의 각각의 단계는 본서 한 권과 듣기 파일로 이루어져 있습니다. 각각의 책은 12개의 장으로 구성되어 있으며, 각 장은 2-4개의 관련된 단원들로 구성되어 있습니다. 각 책은 또한 다양하면서 독특하고 재미있는 주제를 다루고 있으며, 영어 실력 수준이 다양한 학생들의 요구를 충족시킬 수 있는 적절한 길이와 깊이로 나누어져 있습니다.

각 단원을 학습한 후에, 여러분은 관련된 문제와 연습문제들을 통해서 단어와 표현들을 복습할 수 있습니다. 또한, MP3 음성 파일의 대본을 들을 수 있습니다. 이 시리즈가 여러분이 좀 더 능숙한 영어 실력자로 되기 위한 도약의 발판으로 도움이 될 수 있기를 바랍니다. 스토리텔링 보카강사 되다! 가 여러분의 영어 실력의 향상을 도와줄 수 있다고 확신합니다.

## Structure

- **Reading Passages**

  이 파트는 10대의 삶에서부터 사회적인 이슈 범위까지, 다양한 주제들을 다룹니다. 지문 속의 각각의 문장은 배워야 할 목표 단어들을 포함하고 있습니다. 각각의 인물은 자신만의 성격을 가지고 있으며, 현실적인 주제들이 지문을 좀 더 쉽게 이해할 수 있도록 도와줄 것입니다. 또한, 이 파트는 여러분이 지문 속에서 사용된 어휘들을 자신감을 느끼고 배울 수 있도록 동기부여 해 줄 것입니다.

- **Words**

  영어로 단어의 뜻을 읽기를 권장합니다. 그렇게 하는 것이 영어 단어를 학습할 수 있는 더 많은 기회를 제공합니다. 또한, 목표 어휘와 더불어 단어의 어원과 활용 문장을 읽기를 권장합니다.

- **Check Again!**

  이 파트는 각각의 단원들에서 학습한 단어들과 관용구를 다양한 접근으로 연습해 볼 기회를 제공합니다.

- **Voca Plus**

  이 파트는 각각의 장의 마지막으로, 각 장의 내용과 관련된 기본 단어들과 사진들을 보여줍니다. 또한, 각 장과 관련된 문화 팁도 함께 포함하고 있습니다.

# Contents

### Chapter 1. Teen Life ...8
Unit 1  Is that you, mom? ...**10**
Unit 2  Seri is smart. ...**16**

### Chapter 2. My home and Neighborhood ...24
Unit 3  Hoony is my bad little brother. ...**26**
Unit 4  I can't find Sujin's address. ...**32**

**Bomi**
A middle school student
An inquisitive teenage girl

### Chapter 3. Learning ...40
Unit 5  I had a history test. ...**42**
Unit 6  What a shame! ...**48**

### Chapter 4. Trips and Entertainment ...56
Unit 7  Seri and I were on a magic carpet! ...**58**
Unit 8  Hoony is at a folk village. ...**64**
Unit 9  My aunt went to India for a holiday. ...**70**

**Hoony**
Bomi's younger brother

### Chapter 5. Hobbies ...78
Unit 10  Welcome Danny! ...**80**
Unit 11  It was such a long day. ...**86**
Unit 12  Knitting doesn't suit me. ...**92**

### Chapter 6. Health ...100
Unit 13  I had the mumps. ...**102**
Unit 14  I want fried chicken. ...**108**

**Seri**
Bomi's younger sister

**Sara**
Bomi's best friend

**Mom**
Bomi, Hoony, and Seri's mother

**Dad**
Bomi, Hoony, and Seri's father

### Chapter 7. People ...116

Unit 15  Our teacher became an April Fool. ...**118**
Unit 16  Dad, don't forget your New Year's resolutions. ...**124**
Unit 17  I envy Sujin's aunt. ...**130**
Unit 18  I remember the first day we met. ...**136**

### Chapter 8. History, Art, and Culture ...144

Unit 19  Seri designed her own bandage. ...**146**
Unit 20  Hoony has a bubble show. ...**152**
Unit 21  Grandpa explained some historical changes. ...**158**

### Chapter 9. Politics and Social Issues ...166

Unit 22  My family volunteered at the ocean village. ...**168**
Unit 23  Seri will design school uniforms for girls. ...**174**
Unit 24  We add some lines to a song. ...**180**

### Chapter 10. Economy ...188

Unit 25  We discuss how to save money. ...**190**
Unit 26  Good job, Brownie! ...**196**
Unit 27  Sorry, Seri! ...**202**

### Chapter 11. Technology ...210

Unit 28  Sara and I are at a robot contest. ...**212**
Unit 29  Grandma belongs to the Internet fishing community. ...**218**

### Chapter 12. Nature and Space ...226

Unit 30  We need to reduce garbage. ...**228**
Unit 31  We're thinking of going on a balloon ride. ...**234**
Unit 32  We had a good time. ...**240**

# STORYTELLING VOCABULARY

## GREEN

## Chapter 1. Teen Life

Unit 1. Is that you, mom?

Unit 2. Seri is smart.

# Chapter 1
# Teen Life

Unit 1. Is that you, mom?

freeze in a thin dress

have a crush on someone

not **look embarrassed**

# Episode

Dear Mom,

Mom, I found your **wedding** pictures. • I can't **believe** it's really you. • You **looked** like a model. • You were so **slim** and beautiful! • Did dad have a **crush** on you? • Or did someone **introduce** you? • How did he ask you to **marry** him?

Wow, are those my **grandparents**? • So many people were **invited** to the wedding! • You were **shaking**, weren't you? • Was it **because** you were **nervous**? • Or were you **freezing** in that **thin** dress? • I see you had a big **party**. • Why was dad **wearing** your high heels? • Did he **lose** his **shoes**? • But he didn't look very **embarrassed**.

---

엄마에게,

엄마, 엄마의 결혼식 사진들을 찾았어요. 정말 엄마라는 게 안 믿어져요. 엄마는 모델 같아 보였어요. 아주 날씬하고 아름다웠어요. 아빠가 엄마에게 반했어요? 아니면 누군가가 아빠와 엄마를 소개시켜 주었어요? 아빠가 엄마에게 어떻게 청혼했어요?

와, 이분들이 할아버지, 할머니세요? 결혼식에 아주 많은 사람들이 초대되었군요! 엄마는 떨고 있었죠, 그렇죠? 긴장해서 그런 거였어요? 아니면 그 얇은 드레스를 입고 추워서 그랬어요? 큰 파티를 했었나 봐요. 아빠가 왜 엄마의 하이힐을 신고 있었어요? 신발을 잃어버렸나요? 하지만 아빠는 그다지 창피해 보이지 않았어요.

## wedding
[wédiŋ]
n. 결혼식

Mom, I found your wedding pictures.
엄마, 엄마의 결혼식 사진들을 찾았어요.

## believe
[bilíːv]
v. 믿다

I can't believe it's really you.
정말 당신이라는 게 안 믿어져요.
- belief  n. 믿음
- believe - believed - believed

## look
[lúk]
v. 보다, 보이다

You looked like a model.
당신은 모델 같아 보였어요.
- look like  ~처럼 보이다
- look - looked - looked

## slim
[slím]
a. 날씬한, 가는

You were so slim and beautiful!
당신은 아주 날씬하고 아름다웠어요.

## crush
[kráʃ]
n. 홀딱 반함

Did dad have a crush on you?
아빠가 당신에게 반했어요?
- have a crush on  ~에게 홀딱 반하다

## introduce
[ìntrədjúːs]
v. 소개하다, 만나게 해주다

Or did someone introduce you?
아니면 누군가가 두 사람을 소개시켜 주었어요?
- introduction  n. 소개
- introduce - introduced - introduced

## marry
[mǽri]
v. ~와 결혼하다

How did he ask you to marry him?
그가 당신에게 어떻게 청혼했어요?
- marriage  n. 결혼
- marry - married - married

## grandparent
[grǽndpɛ̀ərənt]
n. 조부모

Wow, are those my grandparents?
와, 이분들이 우리 할아버지, 할머니세요?

## invite
[inváit]
v. 초대하다

So many people were invited to the wedding!
결혼식에 아주 많은 사람들이 초대되었군요!
- invitation  n. 초대
- invite - invited - invited

## shake
[ʃéik]
v. 떨다, 흔들다

You were shaking, weren't you?
당신은 떨고 있었죠, 그렇죠?
- shake - shook - shaken

## because
[bikɔ́ːz]
con. ~때문에

Was it because you were nervous?
긴장해서 그런 거였어요?

## nervous
[nə́ːrvəs]
a. 긴장한, 불안한

Was it because you were nervous?
긴장해서 그런 거였어요?
- nervously  ad. 신경질적으로, 초조하게

## freeze
[fríːz]
v. 얼다

Or were you freezing in that thin dress?
아니면 그 얇은 드레스를 입고 추워서 그랬어요?
- freezing  a. 어는, 몹시 추운   • frozen  a. 언
- freeze - froze - frozen

## thin
[θín]
a. 얇은, 가는

Or were you freezing in that thin dress?
아니면 그 얇은 드레스를 입고 추워서 그랬어요?

## party
[páːrti]
n. 파티

I see you had a big party.
큰 파티를 했었나 봐요.
- have a party  파티를 열다

## wear
[wɛ́ər]
v. ~을 입다, 신다

Why was dad wearing your high heels?
아빠가 왜 당신의 하이힐을 신고 있었어요?
- wear - wore - worn

## lose
[lúːz]
v. ~을 잃다

Did he lose his shoes?
그는 신발을 잃어버렸나요?
- loss  n. 손실, 손해
- lose - lost - lost

## shoes
[ʃúːz]
n. 신발, 구두

Did he lose his shoes?
그는 신발을 잃어버렸나요?

## embarrassed
[imbǽrəst]
a. 창피한, 무안한

But he didn't look very embarrassed.
하지만 그는 그다지 창피해 보이지 않았어요.
- embarrass  v. 무안하게 하다, 난처하게 하다
- embarrassment  n. 당황, 난처

# Check Again!

**A** Translate each word or expression into Korean.

1. wedding .................................
2. believe .................................
3. look like .................................
4. slim .................................
5. introduce .................................
6. grandparent .................................
7. because .................................
8. shake .................................
9. freeze .................................
10. embarrassed .................................

**B** Translate each word or expression into English.

1. 얇은, 가는 .................................
2. 초대하다 .................................
3. 긴장한, 불안한 .................................
4. ~을 입다, 신다 .................................
5. 파티를 열다 .................................

**C** Fill in the blank with the appropriate word. Refer to the Korean.

1. The little boy promised to m_____ the little girl someday.
   꼬마 남자아이는 언젠가는 그 꼬마 여자아이와 결혼하기로 약속했어요.

2. I think my brother has a c_____ on you.
   내 오빠가 너한테 홀딱 반한 것 같아.

3. Tim l_____ his shoes at a Korean BBQ restaurant.
   팀은 한국 바비큐 레스토랑에서 신발을 잃어버렸어요.

4. Could you i_____ me to your cute friend?
   너의 귀여운 친구에게 나를 소개해 줄 수 있니?

5. Sara was e_____ when she saw a hole in her socks.
   사라는 양말에 있는 구멍을 보고 창피해 했어요.

# Chapter 1
# Teen Life

Unit 2. Seri is smart.

**be rude**

**act polite**

**print out** some pictures

**cook ramen**

# Episode

Dear Diary,

Mom and dad are **away** right now. • They went to an apple **festival**. • So I am **free** to do whatever I want. • Now is my **chance**! • I want to **teach** Seri a **lesson**. • She is always so **rude** to me. • But she acts **polite** to me **in front of** mom and dad. • I will tell her, "**Turn** on the computer and printer. • **Print** out some pictures for me." • I know she won't **listen** to me.

What a **surprise**! • Seri is **obeying** me. • She is **boiling** water. • She is even **cooking** ramen for me. • She says she is using her own **recipe**. • It **smells** wonderful. • She also brings cold water on a **tray**. • Seri, you realize that I'm the **boss** right now. • You are pretty **smart**!

---

다이어리에게,
엄마와 아빠는 지금 멀리 떠나 계셔. 그들은 사과 축제에 가셨어. 그래서 나는 내가 원하는 것은 뭐든지 할 수 있어. 이때가 내 기회인 거야! 나는 세리에게 버릇을 가르쳐주고 싶어. 세리는 항상 나에게 무례해. 하지만 엄마와 아빠 앞에서는 나에게 공손하게 행동해. "컴퓨터와 프린터를 켜. 나에게 사진을 몇 장 출력해 줘"라고 말할 거야. 세리가 내 말을 듣지 않을 걸 알아.
아주 뜻밖이야! 세리가 내 말을 잘 듣고 있어. 세리가 물을 끓이고 있어. 심지어 나를 위해 라면을 끓이고 있어. 세리는 자기만의 요리법을 사용하고 있다고 말해. 아주 좋은 냄새가 나. 세리는 시원한 물을 쟁반 위에 올려서 가져와. 세리, 너는 내가 지금 대장이라는 걸 아는구나. 너는 정말 눈치가 빨라!

## away
[əwéi]
ad. 멀리 떨어져서

Mom and dad are away right now.
엄마와 아빠는 지금 멀리 떠나 계셔.

## festival
[féstəvəl]
n. 축제

They went to an apple festival.
그들은 사과 축제에 가셨어.

## free
[fríː]
a. 자유로운

So I am free to do whatever I want.
그래서 나는 내가 원하는 것은 뭐든지 할 수 있어.
- free to + V  자유로이 ~할 수 있는
- freedom  n. 자유, 해방

## chance
[tʃæns]
n. 기회

Now is my chance!
이때가 내 기회인 거야!

## teach
[tíːtʃ]
v. ~를 가르치다

I want to teach Seri a lesson.
나는 세리에게 버릇을 가르쳐주고 싶어.
- teach ~ a lesson  v. ~에게 교훈을 주다, ~에게 버릇을 가르치다
- teach - taught - taught

## lesson
[lésn]
n. 훈계, 수업, 교훈

I want to teach Seri a lesson.
나는 세리에게 버릇을 가르쳐주고 싶어.

## rude
[rúːd]
a. 무례한

She is always so rude to me.
그녀는 항상 나에게 무례해.
- rudely  ad. 버릇없이, 무례하게

## polite
[pəláit]
a. 공손한, 예의바른

But she acts polite to me in front of mom and dad.
하지만 엄마와 아빠 앞에서는 나에게 공손하게 행동해.

## in front of
[in fránt ɔv]
~의 앞에(서)

But she acts polite to me in front of mom and dad.
하지만 엄마와 아빠 앞에서는 나에게 공손하게 행동해.

## turn
[tə́ːrn]
v. 돌리다

I will tell her, "Turn on the computer and printer. Print out some pictures for me."
나는 "컴퓨터와 프린터를 켜. 나에게 사진을 몇 장 출력해 줘."라고 말할 거야.

- turn on (불, 전등 등을) 켜다 · turn off (불, 전등 등을) 끄다
- turn - turned - turned

## print
[prínt]
v. 인쇄하다

I will tell her, "Turn on the computer and printer. Print out some pictures for me."
나는 "컴퓨터와 프린터를 켜. 나에게 사진을 몇 장 출력해 줘."라고 말할 거야.

- print out 출력하다
- print - printed - printed

## listen
[lísən]
v. 듣다

I know she won't listen to me.
그녀가 내 말을 듣지 않을 걸 알아.

- listen to ~을 듣다
- listen - listened - listened

## surprise
[sərpráiz]
n. 놀랄 만한 사건, 뜻밖의 일

What a surprise!
아주 뜻밖이야!

- surprising a. 놀라운 · surprised a. 놀란

## obey
[oubéi]
v. 복종하다, 말을 잘 듣다

Seri is obeying me.
세리가 내 말을 잘 듣고 있어.

- obedience n. 순종 · obedient a. 순종하는
- obey - obeyed - obeyed

## boil
[bɔ́il]
v. 끓이다

She is boiling water.
그녀가 물을 끓이고 있어.
- boil - boiled - boiled

## cook
[kúk]
v. 요리하다  n. 요리사

She is even cooking ramen for me.
그녀는 심지어 나를 위해 라면을 끓이고 있어.
- cook - cooked - cooked

## recipe
[résəpìː]
n. 조리법, 요리법

She says she is using her own recipe.
그녀는 자기만의 요리법을 사용하고 있다고 말해.

## smell
[smél]
v. 냄새가 나다

It smells wonderful.
그것은 아주 좋은 냄새가 나.
- smell - smelled - smelled

## tray
[tréi]
n. 쟁반

She also brings cold water on a tray.
그녀는 시원한 물을 쟁반 위에 올려서 가져와.

## boss
[bɔ́(ː)s]
n. 두목, 대장

Seri, you realize that I'm the boss right now.
세리, 너는 내가 지금 대장이라는 걸 아는구나.

## smart
[smáːrt]
a. 눈치 빠른, 영리한

You are pretty smart!
너는 정말 눈치가 빨라!

# Check Again!

**A** Translate each word or expression into Korean.

1. festival ..................  2. free ..................
3. recipe ..................  4. polite ..................
5. tray ..................  6. print out ..................
7. listen to ..................  8. cook ..................
9. in front of ..................  10. boss ..................

**B** Translate each word or expression into English.

1. 기회 ..................
2. 무례한 ..................
3. 눈치 빠른, 영리한 ..................
4. 뜻밖의 일 ..................
5. 끓이다 ..................

**C** Fill in the blank with the appropriate word. Refer to the Korean.

1. A friend called while you were a_____.
   당신이 없을 때 친구한테서 전화가 왔어요.

2. Does my hair s_____ bad?
   내 머리에서 좋지 않은 냄새나요?

3. That will t_____ him a lesson!
   그러면 그의 버릇이 좀 고쳐지겠죠!

4. Who t_____ on this computer?
   누가 이 컴퓨터를 켰어요?

5. He always o_____ his parents.
   그는 항상 부모님의 말씀을 잘 따라요.

Chapter 1. Teen Life

Voca Plus!

# Family tree

1. Mr. Cohen
2. Mrs. Cohen
3. Betty
4. James
5. Sarah
6. Chuck
7. Nick
8. Kathy
9. Brian
10. Elizabeth
11. Harry

- ①② **grandparent** 조부모
- ③ **mother** 엄마
- ④ **father** 아빠
- ⑤ **aunt** 고모 (이모, 숙모)
- ⑥ **uncle** 고모부 (이모부, 삼촌)
- ⑦⑧ **cousin** 사촌
- ⑨ **brother** 형 (오빠, 남동생)
- ⑩ **sister** 누나 (언니, 여동생)

Mrs. Cohen is Mr. Cohen's **wife** and Mr. Cohen is Mrs. Cohen's **husband**.
코헨 여사는 코헨 씨의 부인이고 코헨 씨는 코헨 여사의 남편입니다.

James is Mr. Cohen's **son** and Sarah is Mr. Cohen's **daughter**.
제임스는 코헨 씨의 아들이고 사라는 코헨 씨의 딸입니다.

Betty is Mrs. Cohen's **daughter-in-law** and Chuck is Mrs. Cohen's **son-in-law**.
베티는 코헨 여사의 며느리이고 척은 코헨 여사의 사위입니다.

Brian is Nick's **cousin** and Kathy is Elizabeth's **cousin**.
브라이언은 닉의 사촌이고 캐시는 엘리자베스의 사촌입니다.

The Cohens are Elizabeth's and Harry's **grandparents**.
코헨 씨 부부는 엘리자베스와 해리의 조부모님입니다.

Nick is James' **nephew** and Kathy is James' **niece**.
닉은 제임스의 조카이고 캐시는 제임스의 조카딸입니다.

Sarah is Brian's **aunt** and Chuck is Brian's **uncle**.
사라는 브라이언의 고모이고 척은 브라이언의 고모부입니다.

## Culture Plus

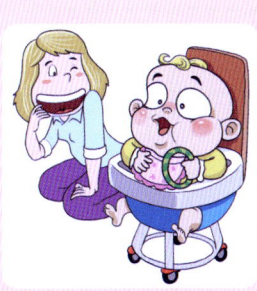

**Baby's room** 아기 방

+ mobile 모빌
+ blanket 담요
+ diaper 기저귀
+ milk bottle 우유병
+ walker 보행기
+ stroller 유모차
+ swing 그네
+ high chair 유아용 의자
+ cradle 요람

# STORYTELLING VOCABULARY

GREEN

## Chapter 2. My home and Neighborhood

**Unit 3.** Hoony is my bad little brother.

**Unit 4.** I can't find Sujin's address.

# Chapter 2
# My home and Neighborhood

Unit 3. Hoony is my bad little brother.

**make** bang-bang **noises**

**try to choke** someone

**spill water** on the carpet

**take** a robot **apart**

# Episode

Dear Hoony,

You make our home so **special**, Hoony. • I'm trying to **relax** in my room. • But you come in making bang-bang **noises**. • Get out of here with your **toy gun**! • I'm not **deaf**. • I'm reading a **comic book** on the sofa. • Hey, what are you doing to my **scarf**? • Stop **pulling** at it. • Are you trying to **choke** me? • Oh, you're so **careless**! • You **spilled** water on the **carpet**. • And what are these **pieces** on the kitchen floor? • Did you **take** your robot apart? • Come on, let's **collect** them together.

You are not **blind**, are you? • Look, your room is so **messy**. • Your socks are **lying everywhere**. • Was I this bad at your **age**? • Socks go in the **drawer**.

---

후니에게,

후니, 너는 우리 집을 정말 특별하게 만들어. 나는 내 방에서 쉬려고 해. 그런데 네가 빵빵 소리를 내며 들어와. 장난감 총을 가지고 여기서 나가 줘! 나는 귀머거리가 아니야. 나는 소파에 앉아 만화책을 보고 있어. 이봐, 내 목도리를 가지고 뭐하는 거야? 그것을 그만 잡아당겨. 나를 숨막히게 하려는 거야? 아, 너는 정말 조심성이 없구나! 카펫 위에 물을 엎질렀잖아. 그리고 부엌 바닥에 놓인 이 조각들은 뭐니? 네 로봇을 분해했니? 자, 조각들을 함께 모으자. 너는 장님이 아니잖아, 그렇지? 봐, 네 방은 정말 지저분해. 네 양말은 사방에 놓여 있어. 나도 네 나이에 이렇게 행동했을까? 양말은 서랍에 들어가야지.

## special
[spéʃəl]
a. 특별한

You make our home so special, Hoony.
후니, 너는 우리 집을 정말 특별하게 만들어.
- specialize  v. 특수화하다, 전문화하다

## relax
[rilǽks]
v. 쉬다

I'm trying to relax in my room.
나는 내 방에서 쉬려고 해.
- relaxation  n. 편히 쉼, 기분 전환
- relax - relaxed - relaxed

## noise
[nɔ́iz]
n. 소음

But you come in making bang-bang noises.
그런데 네가 빵빵 소리를 내며 들어와.
- noisy  a. 시끄러운  • make a noise  떠들다

## toy gun
[tɔ́i gʌ̀n]
장난감 총

Get out of here with your toy gun!
장난감 총을 가지고 여기서 나가 줘!

## deaf
[déf]
a. 귀머거리의, 귀가 먼

I'm not deaf.
나는 귀머거리가 아니야.

## comic book
[kɔ́mik bùk]
만화책

I'm reading a comic book on the sofa.
나는 소파에 앉아 만화책을 보고 있어.

## scarf
[skɑ́ːrf]
n. 목도리

Hey, what are you doing to my scarf?
이봐, 내 목도리를 가지고 뭐하는 거야?

## pull
[púl]
v. 잡아당기다

Stop pulling at it.
그것을 그만 잡아당겨.
- pull - pulled - pulled

## choke
[tʃóuk]
v. 숨막히게 하다

Are you trying to choke me?
나를 숨막히게 하려는 거야?
- choke - choked - choked

## careless
[kɛ́ərlis]
a. 부주의한, 조심성 없는

Oh, you're so careless!
아, 너는 정말 조심성이 없구나!
- care  n. 조심, 염려
- carelessness  n. 부주의, 경솔

## spill
[spíl]
v. 엎지르다

You spilled water on the carpet.
카펫 위에 물을 엎질렀잖아.
- spill - spilled/spilt - spilled/spilt

## carpet
[káːrpit]
n. 카펫, 양탄자

You spilled water on the carpet.
카펫 위에 물을 엎질렀잖아.

## piece
[píːs]
n. 조각

And what are these pieces on the kitchen floor?
그리고 부엌 바닥에 놓인 이 조각들은 뭐야?

## take
[téik]
v. 잡다, 가지고 가다

Did you take your robot apart?
네 로봇을 분해했니?
- take apart  분해하다
- take - took - taken

## collect
[kəlékt]
v. 모으다

Come on, let's collect them together.
자, 조각들을 함께 모으자.
- collection   n. 수집   • collective   a. 집합적인
- collect - collected - collected

## blind
[bláind]
a. 눈 먼, 장님인

You are not blind, are you?
너는 장님이 아니잖아, 그렇지?

## messy
[mési]
a. 지저분한, 어질러진

Look, your room is so messy.
봐, 네 방은 정말 지저분해.
- mess   n. 뒤죽박죽, 어질러놓은 것

## lie
[lái]
v. 놓여 있다

Your socks are lying everywhere.
네 양말은 사방에 놓여 있어.
- lie - lay - lain

## everywhere
[évrihwɛ̀ər]
ad. 어디에나, 도처에

Your socks are lying everywhere.
네 양말은 사방에 놓여 있어.

## age
[éidʒ]
n. 나이

Was I this bad at your age?
나도 네 나이에 이렇게 행동했을까?
- aged   a. 늙은, ~나이의

## drawer
[drɔ́:ər]
n. 서랍

Socks go in the drawer.
양말은 서랍에 들어가야지.

# Check Again!

**A** Translate each word or expression into Korean.

1. relax ..................................  2. everywhere ..................................
3. comic book ..........................  4. scarf ..................................
5. pull ..................................  6. choke ..................................
7. careless ..............................  8. piece ..................................
9. collect ..............................  10. messy ..................................

**B** Translate each word or expression into English.

1. 특별한 ..................................
2. 눈 먼, 장님인 ..................................
5. 서랍 ..................................
4. 놓여 있다 ..................................
3. 귀머거리의, 귀가 먼 ..................................

**C** Fill in the blank with the appropriate word. Refer to the Korean.

1. Dad took the phone a_____.
   아빠는 전화기를 분해했어요.

2. Jack made funny n_____ with his lips.
   잭은 입술로 이상한 소리를 냈어요.

3. Alice s_____ milk on her shirt.
   앨리스는 셔츠에 우유를 엎질렀어요.

4. What's that l_____ on your desk?
   네 책상 위에 있는 저것은 뭐니?

5. Don't ask her about her a_____.
   그녀에게 나이를 묻지 말아요.

# Chapter 2
# My home and Neighborhood

Unit 4. I can't find Sujin's address.

**miss** one's stop

**ask for directions**

be **just in time** for cake

# Episode

Sara: Bomi! Why weren't you at the **subway station**?

Bomi: I **missed** my stop and had to come back. • How could you leave **without** me?

Sara: Sorry, but I knew you had Sujin's **address**.

Bomi: But I didn't know the **location**! • I went into a **bakery** and asked the man for **directions**. • He said I would see a **bookstore** and I should **turn** right there. • Well, I saw a big **church**. • Then I saw a big **supermarket**, but no bookstore.

Sara: But it's right **next to** the supermarket.

Bomi: I thought I **passed** by it too. • So I **quickly** made a **U-turn**. • **Luckily**, I found the bookstore this time. • I found Sujin's place **across** from the bookstore.

Sara: Well, you're **just in time** for cake!

---

사라: 보미! 너 왜 지하철역에 없었니?
보미: 정거장을 놓쳐서 되돌아와야 했어. 어떻게 나 없이 떠날 수가 있었니?
사라: 미안해, 하지만 네가 수진의 주소를 가지고 있다고 알고 있었어.
보미: 하지만 위치는 몰랐단 말이야! 나는 제과점에 들어가서 그곳 남자에게 길을 물었어. 그는 내가 서점을 보게 될 거고 거기에서 오른쪽으로 돌아야 한다고 말했어. 그런데, 나는 큰 교회를 봤어. 그리고 대형 슈퍼마켓을 봤지만 서점은 못 봤어.
사라: 그곳은 슈퍼마켓 바로 옆에 있는데.
보미: 나도 그곳을 지나쳤다고 생각했어. 그래서 나는 재빠르게 되돌아왔지. 다행히도 이번에는 서점을 찾았어. 나는 서점 맞은편 수진의 집을 찾았어.
사라: 아무튼, 케이크 먹을 때 딱 맞춰 왔네!

| | |
|---|---|
| **subway station**<br>[sʌ́bwèi stéiʃən]<br>지하철역 | Bomi! Why weren't you at the subway station?<br>보미! 너 왜 지하철역에 없었니? |
| **miss**<br>[mís]<br>v. 놓치다 | I missed my stop and had to come back.<br>나는 정거장을 놓쳐서 되돌아와야 했어.<br>• miss - missed - missed |
| **without**<br>[wiðáut]<br>prep. ~이 없이 | How could you leave without me?<br>어떻게 나 없이 떠날 수가 있었니? |
| **address**<br>[ǽdres]<br>n. 주소, 연설 | Sorry, but I knew you had Sujin's address.<br>미안해, 하지만 네가 수진의 주소를 가지고 있다고 알고 있었어. |
| **location**<br>[loukéiʃən]<br>n. 위치 | But I didn't know the location!<br>하지만 나는 위치를 몰랐단 말이야! |
| **bakery**<br>[béikəri]<br>n. 제과점 | I went into a bakery and asked the man for directions.<br>나는 제과점에 들어가서 그곳 남자에게 길을 물었어. |

## direction
[dirékʃən]
n. 방향

I went into a bakery and asked the man for directions.
나는 제과점에 들어가서 그곳 남자에게 길을 물었어.

- ask for directions 길을 묻다

## bookstore
[búkstɔ̀ːr]
n. 서점

He said I would see a bookstore and I should turn right there.
그는 내가 서점을 보게 될 거고 거기에서 오른쪽으로 돌아야 한다고 말했어.

## turn
[tə́ːrn]
v. 돌다

He said I would see a bookstore and I should turn right there.
그는 내가 서점을 보게 될 거고 거기에서 오른쪽으로 돌아야 한다고 말했어.

- turn right 오른쪽으로 돌다, 우회전하다
- turn left 왼쪽으로 돌다, 좌회전하다
- turn - turned - turned

## church
[tʃə́ːrtʃ]
n. 교회

Well, I saw a big church.
그런데, 나는 큰 교회를 봤어.

## supermarket
[súːpərmὰːrkit]
n. 슈퍼마켓

Then I saw a big supermarket, but no bookstore.
그리고 나는 대형 슈퍼마켓을 봤지만 서점은 못 봤어.

## next to
[nékst tuː]
~의 옆에

But it's right next to the supermarket.
그곳은 슈퍼마켓 바로 옆에 있어.

Chapter 2. My home and Neighborhood

## pass
[pǽs]
v. 지나가다, 통과하다

I thought I passed by it too.
나도 그곳을 지나쳤다고 생각했어.
- pass by  지나치다
- pass - passed - passed

## quickly
[kwíkli]
ad. 빨리, 속히

So I quickly made a U-turn.
그래서 나는 재빠르게 되돌아왔지.
- quick  a. 빠른, 신속한

## U-turn
[júː-tèːrn]
n. U턴, 회전

So I quickly made a U-turn.
그래서 나는 재빠르게 되돌아왔지.

## luckily
[lʌ́kili]
ad. 다행히도

Luckily, I found the bookstore this time.
다행히도 이번에는 서점을 찾았어.

## across
[əkrɔ́ːs]
prep. ~을 가로질러

I found Sujin's place across from the bookstore.
나는 서점 맞은편 수진의 집을 찾았어.
- across from  ~의 맞은편에

## just in time
[dʒʌ́st in tàim]
때맞추어

Well, you're just in time for cake!
아무튼, 케이크 먹을 때 딱 맞춰 왔네!

# Check Again!

**A** Translate each word or expression into Korean.

1. luckily ........................
2. address ........................
3. location ........................
4. direction ........................
5. church ........................
6. next to ........................
7. pass ........................
8. across from ........................
9. subway station ........................
10. just in time ........................

**B** Translate each word or expression into English.

1. ~을 가로질러 ........................
2. 빨리, 속히 ........................
3. 서점 ........................
4. 지나치다 ........................
5. 길을 묻다 ........................

**C** Fill in the blank with the appropriate word. Refer to the Korean.

1. A new s_____ opened on our street.
   우리 길에 새로운 슈퍼마켓이 개업했어요.

2. I can't live w_____ my MP3 player.
   나는 내 MP3 플레이어 없이는 못 살아.

3. You gave that man the wrong d_____!
   너는 그 남자에게 길을 잘못 알려줬어!

4. Please t_____ right at the next light.
   다음 신호등에서 우회전해 주세요.

5. I got up late and m_____ the school bus.
   나는 늦게 일어나서 스쿨버스를 놓쳤어요.

# My neighborhood

1. school 학교
2. bus stop 버스정류소
3. fire station 소방서
4. gas station 주유소
5. hospital 병원
6. supermarket 슈퍼마켓
7. restaurant 식당
8. crosswalk 횡단보도
9. intersection 교차로
10. overpass 육교
11. kindergarten 유치원
12. bookstore 서점
13. convenience store 편의점

- There is a restaurant **on the corner of** the road.
  길 모퉁이에 식당이 있습니다.

- There is a supermarket **in front of** the overpass.
  육교 앞에 슈퍼마켓이 있습니다.

- There is a gas station **behind** the hospital.
  병원 뒤에 주유소가 있습니다.

- There is a gas station **next to** the fire station.
  소방서 옆에 주유소가 있습니다.

- There is an intersection **by** the hospital.
  병원 근처에 교차로가 있습니다.

- There is a fire station **across from** the kindergarten.
  유치원 맞은 편에 소방서가 있습니다.

- There is a convenience store **between** the bookstore and the gas station.
  서점과 주유소 사이에 편의점이 있습니다.

*Culture Plus*

**My room** 방

- light 등
- closet 붙박이 옷장
- window 창문
- rug 깔개
- armchair 안락의자
- couch 소파
- picture 액자, 그림
- ceiling 천장
- chest of drawers 옷장

# STORYTELLING VOCABULARY

## GREEN

## Chapter 3. Learning

Unit 5. I had a history test.

Unit 6. What a shame!

# Chapter 3
# Learning

Unit 5. I had a history test.

be popular with the girls

be bad at memorizing

get a good grade

# Episode

Dear Diary,

Do you know what my favorite **subject** is? • It's **history**. • I like Mr. Choi, our history **teacher**. • He is so **good-looking**. • And his voice is so **charming**. • He is very **popular** with the girls.

This morning I had a history **test**. • I read the **textbook**. • And I **reviewed** it about five times. • But I'm so bad at **memorizing**. • Mom **praised** me. • She said, "You're making an **effort**. • I'm **proud of** you." • I got my **lucky** pen and went to school.

I **arrived** at school a little early. • And I kept **preparing** for the test. • Then our history teacher, Mr. Choi walked in. • I hope I get a good **grade**. • I don't want to **disappoint** him.

---

다이어리에게,
너는 내가 가장 좋아하는 과목이 무엇인지 아니? 그건 역사야. 나는 우리 역사 선생님인 최 선생님을 좋아해. 그는 아주 잘생겼어. 그리고 목소리는 아주 매력적이야. 그는 여자아이들 사이에서 아주 인기 있어.
오늘 아침에 나는 역사 시험이 있었어. 나는 교과서를 읽었어. 그리고 나는 그것을 다섯 번이나 복습했어. 그렇지만 나는 암기를 정말 못해. 엄마는 나를 칭찬해줬어. 나에게 "노력하고 있구나. 나는 네가 자랑스럽단다"라고 말씀하셨어. 나는 내 행운의 펜을 챙겨 학교로 갔어.
나는 학교에 조금 일찍 도착했어. 그리고 나는 계속 시험 준비를 했어. 그때 우리 역사 선생님인 최 선생님이 들어오셨어. 나는 좋은 점수를 받았으면 좋겠어. 나는 그를 실망시키고 싶지 않아.

## subject
[sʌ́bdʒikt]
n. 과목

Do you know what my favorite subject is?
너는 내가 가장 좋아하는 과목이 무엇인지 아니?

## history
[hístəri]
n. 역사

It's history.
그건 역사야.

## teacher
[tíːtʃər]
n. 선생님

I like Mr. Choi, our history teacher.
나는 우리 역사 선생님인 최 선생님을 좋아해.

## good-looking
[gúdlúkiŋ]
a. 잘생긴

He is so good-looking.
그는 아주 잘생겼어.

## charming
[tʃáːrmiŋ]
a. 매력적인

And his voice is so charming.
그리고 그의 목소리는 아주 매력적이야.
- charm  n. 매력

## popular
[pápjələr]
a. 인기 있는

He is very popular with the girls.
그는 여자아이들 사이에서 아주 인기 있어.
- popularity  n. 인기
- be popular with  ~ 사이에 인기가 있다

## test
[tést]
n. 테스트

This morning I had a history test.
오늘 아침에 나는 역사 시험이 있었어.

## textbook
[tékstbùk]
n. 교과서

I read the textbook.
나는 교과서를 읽었어.

## review
[rivjúː]
v. 복습하다 n. 복습

And I reviewed it about five times.
그리고 나는 그것을 다섯 번이나 복습했어.
- reviewal   n. 재조사, 재검토
- reviewer   n. 비평가, 평론가
- review - reviewed - reviewed

## memorize
[méməràiz]
v. 외우다

But I'm so bad at memorizing.
그렇지만 나는 암기를 정말 못해.
- memory   n. 기억
- be bad(poor) at   ~을 잘 못하다
- memorize - memorized - memorized

## praise
[préiz]
v. 칭찬하다 n. 칭찬

Mom praised me.
엄마는 나를 칭찬해줬어.
- praiseworthy   a. 칭찬할 만한, 훌륭한
- praise - praised - praised

## effort
[éfərt]
n. 노력, 수고

She said, "You're making an effort. I'm proud of you."
"노력하고 있구나. 나는 네가 자랑스럽단다"라고 말씀하셨어.
- make an effort   노력하다

## proud
[práud]
a. 자랑으로 여기는, 자부심이 있는

She said, "You're making an effort. I'm proud of you."
"노력하고 있구나. 나는 네가 자랑스럽단다"라고 말씀하셨어.
- pride  n. 자존심, 자랑거리
- be proud of  ~를 자랑으로 여기다

## lucky
[lʌ́ki]
a. 행운의

I got my lucky pen and went to school.
나는 내 행운의 펜을 챙겨 학교로 갔어.
- luck  n. 행운

## arrive
[əráiv]
v. 도착하다

I arrived at school a little early.
나는 학교에 조금 일찍 도착했어.
- arrival  n. 도착  a. 도착의
- arrive - arrived - arrived

## prepare
[pripɛ́ər]
v. 준비하다

And I kept preparing for the test.
그리고 나는 계속 시험 준비를 했어.
- preparation  n. 준비
- prepare for  ~를 준비하다
- prepare - prepared - prepared

## grade
[gréid]
n. 성적, 평점

I hope I get a good grade.
나는 좋은 점수를 받았으면 좋겠어.

## disappoint
[dìsəpɔ́int]
v. 실망시키다

I don't want to disappoint him.
나는 그를 실망시키고 싶지 않아.
- disappointment  n. 실망
- disappointed  a. 실망한
- disappoint - disappointed - disappointed

# Check Again!

**A** Translate each word or expression into Korean.

1. history ............................
2. praise ............................
3. test ............................
4. good-looking ............................
5. charming ............................
6. lucky ............................
7. disappoint ............................
8. memorize ............................
9. popular ............................
10. review ............................

**B** Translate each word or expression into English.

1. 과목 ............................
2. 교과서 ............................
3. 도착하다 ............................
4. 성적 ............................
5. 선생님 ............................

**C** Fill in the blank with the appropriate word. Refer to the Korean.

1. Who are you p_____ of?
   당신은 누가 자랑스럽습니까?

2. I'm poor at m_____ words.
   나는 단어를 외우는 데 서툴러.

3. She didn't even make an e_____ to catch the ball.
   그녀는 공을 잡으려고 노력하지도 않았어요.

4. His music is p_____ with teenagers.
   그의 음악은 청소년들 사이에 인기가 있어요.

5. Can you help me p_____ for the party?
   파티 준비하는 것을 도와줄 수 있어요?

# Chapter 3
# Learning

Unit 6. What a shame!

be strict

get very sweaty

get scared and duck

What a shame!

# Episode

Dear Diary,

Mr. Park is our **PE** teacher. • He is very **strict**. • It was hot and **sunny** today. • We had a **football game outside**. • I like **indoor** classes better. • It is hard for Mr. Park's **pupils** outside. • He makes us **move** around a lot. • I got very **sweaty**. • Then I had an **idea**. • I asked to be the **goalkeeper**. • That way I wouldn't have to **chase** the ball. • I could just catch the ball and become a **heroine**! • Another **match** began. • Soon the ball **flew** my way. • But I got **scared** and **ducked**. • The other team **scored**. • What a **shame**!

다이어리에게,

박 선생님은 우리의 체육 선생님이야. 그는 매우 엄격해. 오늘은 덥고 맑게 갠 날이었어. 우리는 밖에서 축구 경기를 했어. 나는 실내 수업이 더 좋아. 밖에 있으면 박 선생님의 학생들은 힘들어. 그는 우리를 아주 많이 움직이게 만들어. 나는 땀이 많이 났어. 그때 내게 생각이 하나 떠올랐어. 나는 골키퍼가 되겠다고 요청했어. 그럼 나는 공을 뒤쫓을 필요가 없을 거야. 그냥 공을 잡아서 영웅이 될 수 있어! 또 다른 시합이 시작되었어. 곧 공이 내 쪽으로 날아왔어. 그렇지만 나는 겁이 나서 몸을 휙 숙였어. 상대 팀이 점수를 얻었어. 무슨 망신이람!

## PE
[píːíː]
체육 (physical education)

Mr. Park is our PE teacher.
박 선생님은 우리의 체육 선생님이야.

## strict
[stríkt]
a. 엄격한, 엄한

He is very strict.
그는 매우 엄격해.
- strictly  ad. 엄격히, 엄밀히

## sunny
[sʌ́ni]
a. 맑게 갠, 햇빛 밝은

It was hot and sunny today.
오늘은 덥고 맑게 갠 날이었어.

## football game
[fútbɔːl ɡeim]
축구 경기

We had a football game outside.
우리는 밖에서 축구 경기를 했어.

## outside
[àutsàid]
ad. 밖에, 바깥에  a. 외부의

We had a football game outside.
우리는 밖에서 축구 경기를 했어.

## indoor
[índɔːr]
a. 실내의

I like indoor classes better.
나는 실내 수업이 더 좋아.
- indoors  ad. 실내에서

## pupil
[pjúːpəl]
n. 학생, 제자

It is hard for Mr. Park's pupils outside.
밖에 있으면 박 선생님의 학생들은 힘들어.

## move
[múːv]
v. 움직이다

He makes us move around a lot.
그는 우리를 아주 많이 움직이게 만들어.
- movement  n. 움직임, 이동
- move around  이곳 저곳으로 돌아다니다
- move - moved - moved

## sweaty
[swéti]
a. 땀이 나는

I got very sweaty.
나는 땀이 많이 났어.
- sweat  n. 땀

## idea
[aidíːə]
n. 생각

Then I had an idea.
그때 내게 생각이 하나 떠올랐어.
- ideal  n. 이상  a. 이상적인
- have an idea  생각이 나다

## goalkeeper
[góulkìːpər]
n. 골키퍼

I asked to be the goalkeeper.
나는 골키퍼가 되겠다고 요청했어.

## chase
[tʃéis]
v. 뒤쫓다, 뛰어다니다

That way I wouldn't have to chase the ball.
그럼 나는 공을 뒤쫓을 필요가 없을 거야.
- chase - chased - chased

## heroine
[hérouin]
n. 영웅, 여장부, 여주인공

I could just catch the ball and become a heroine!
나는 그냥 공을 잡아서 영웅이 될 수 있어!
- hero  n. 영웅, 남주인공

### match
[mǽtʃ]
n. 시합, 경기

Another match began.
또 다른 시합이 시작되었어.

### fly
[flái]
v. 날다

Soon the ball flew my way.
곧 공이 내 쪽으로 날아왔어.
- flight  n. 비행, 도주
- fly - flew - flown

### scared
[skɛ́ərd]
a. 겁에 질린, 무서운

But I got scared and ducked.
그렇지만 나는 겁이 나서 몸을 확 숙였어.
- scare  v. 무섭게 하다, 겁을 주다
- scary  a. 무서운

### duck
[dʌ́k]
v. 머리를 홱 숙이다

But I got scared and ducked.
그렇지만 나는 겁이 나서 몸을 확 숙였어.
- duck - ducked - ducked

### score
[skɔ́:r]
v. 득점하다  n. 득점, 점수

The other team scored.
상대 팀이 점수를 얻었어.
- score - scored - scored

### shame
[ʃéim]
n. 부끄러움, 창피
v. 창피를 주다

What a shame!
무슨 망신이람!
- shameful  a. 부끄러운, 치욕적인

# Check Again!

**A** Translate each word or expression into Korean.

1. PE ....................
2. outside ....................
3. duck ....................
4. pupil ....................
5. move ....................
6. sweaty ....................
7. idea ....................
8. chase ....................
9. football game ....................
10. score ....................

**B** Translate each word or expression into English.

1. 맑게 갠 ....................
2. 실내의 ....................
3. 골키퍼 ....................
4. 날다 ....................
5. 겁에 질린 ....................

**C** Fill in the blank with the appropriate word. Refer to the Korean.

1. Her father is very s_____ .
   그녀의 아버지는 매우 엄격하다.

2. She likes to m_____ things around the house.
   그녀는 집 안에서 물건을 이리저리 옮기는 것을 좋아해요.

3. There is a big boxing m_____ on TV tonight.
   오늘 TV에서 중요한 복싱 경기가 중계돼요.

4. Cathy thinks herself a real h_____ .
   캐시는 자기가 정말 영웅이라고 생각한다.

5. I fell on the ice. What a s_____ !
   나는 얼음에서 넘어졌어. 무슨 망신이람!

Chapter 3. Learning

# Voca Plus!

## In a classroom

1. **principal** 교장 선생님
2. **homeroom teacher** 담임선생님
3. **classroom** 교실
4. **desk** 책상
5. **textbook** 교과서
6. **crossword puzzle** 크로스워드퍼즐
7. **chalk** 분필
8. **eraser** 지우개
9. **chalkboard** 칠판
10. **ruler** 자
11. **paper** 종이
12. **computer** 컴퓨터
13. **measuring tape** 줄자
14. **xylophone** 실로폰

- A girl is **using her ruler**.
  한 여학생이 자를 사용하고 있습니다.

- A boy is **using a computer**.
  한 남학생이 컴퓨터를 하고 있습니다.

- A girl is **reading her textbook**.
  한 여학생이 교과서를 읽고 있습니다.

- A boy is **using a measuring tape**.
  한 남학생이 줄자를 사용하고 있어요.

- A boy is **doing a crossword puzzle**.
  한 남학생이 크로스 워드 퍼즐을 하고 있어요.

- The homeroom teacher is **writing on the board**.
  담임 선생님이 칠판에 필기를 하세요.

- The principal is **coming into the classroom**.
  교장 선생님이 교실로 들어오세요.

## Culture Plus

**Subjects** 과목

- math 수학
- English 영어
- science 과학
- history 역사
- social studies 사회
- music 음악
- art 미술
- physical education 체육
- literature 문학
- Korean 국어

Chapter 3. Learning  55

# STORYTELLING VOCABULARY
## GREEN

## Chapter 4. Trips and Entertainment

**Unit 7.** Seri and I were on a magic carpet!

**Unit 8.** Hoony is at a folk village.

**Unit 9.** My aunt went to India for a holiday.

# Chapter 4
# Trips and Entertainmen

## Unit 7. Seri and I were on a magic carpet!

get **free** cotton candy

**be ready to** try every ride

can't ride because of **height**

**fasten** one's seat belt

# Episode

Dear Diary,

I went to an **amusement** park with Seri and Hoony. • We got all-day **passes**. • We even got **free** cotton candy at the ticket office. • We were **ready** to try every **ride**. • Seri wanted to try the **magic** carpet. • So we stood in a long **line** of people. • Finally, it was our **turn**. • But the **safety** guard stopped Hoony. • He couldn't ride because of his **height**. • What a **waste** of time! • I said, "Hoony, please sit on the **bench** and wait for us. • Don't follow **strangers**." • Then we **fastened** our seat belt and **screamed** when the ride started. • We got off but couldn't find Hoony. • He was **missing**. • It was my **mistake** to leave him **alone**. • "What's that?" I said. • There was a **parade**. • A little boy was **following** it. • It was Hoony.

---

다이어리에게,

나는 세리와 후니랑 놀이 공원에 갔어. 우리는 자유 이용권을 샀어. 우리는 매표소에서 무료로 솜사탕도 받았어. 우리는 모든 놀이기구를 탈 준비가 됐어. 세리는 마법 양탄자를 타보고 싶어했어. 그래서 우리는 사람들이 길게 서 있는 곳에 줄을 섰어. 드디어 우리 차례가 왔어. 하지만 안전 요원이 후니를 막았어. 후니는 키 때문에 탈 수 없었어. 완전히 시간 낭비야! 나는 "후니야, 벤치에 앉아서 우리를 기다려. 처음 보는 사람들을 따라가지 마"라고 말했어. 그리고 우리는 안전벨트를 매고 놀이기구가 시작되자 소리를 질렀어. 놀이기구에서 내렸지만 후니를 찾을 수 없었어. 그가 없어진 거야. 후니를 혼자 놔둔 것은 내 실수였어. "저건 뭐지?" 내가 물었어. 행렬이 있었어. 어린 남자아이가 그것을 따라가고 있었어. 바로 후니였어.

## amusement
[əmjúːzmənt]
n. 즐거움, 재미

I went to an amusement park with Seri and Hoony.
나는 세리와 후니랑 놀이 공원에 갔어.
- amuse   v. 즐겁게 하다   • amused   a. 즐거워하는
- amusement park   놀이 공원

## pass
[pǽs]
n. 이용권   v. 지나가다

We got all-day passes.
우리는 자유 이용권을 샀어.

## free
[fríː]
a. 무료의

We even got free cotton candy at the ticket office.
우리는 매표소에서 무료로 솜사탕도 받았어.

## ready
[rédi]
a. 준비가 된

We were ready to try every ride.
우리는 모든 놀이기구를 탈 준비가 됐어.

## ride
[ráid]
n. 놀이기구   v. 타다

We were ready to try every ride.
우리는 모든 놀이기구를 탈 준비가 됐어.

## magic
[mǽdʒik]
n. 마법, 마술

Seri wanted to try the magic carpet.
세리는 마법 양탄자를 타보고 싶어했어.

## line
[láin]
n. 줄

So we stood in a long line of people.
그래서 우리는 사람들이 길게 서 있는 곳에 줄을 섰어.
- stand in line   줄을 서다

## turn
[tə́ːrn]
n. 차례 v. 돌다

Finally, it was our turn.
드디어 우리 차례가 왔어.

## safety
[séifti]
n. 안전

But the safety guard stopped Hoony.
하지만 안전 요원이 후니를 막았어.
- safe　a. 안전한　• safely　ad. 안전하게

## height
[háit]
n. 키

He couldn't ride because of his height.
그는 키 때문에 탈 수 없었어.
- high　a. 높은

## waste
[wéist]
n. 낭비 v. 낭비하다

What a waste of time!
완전히 시간 낭비야!
- wasteful　a. 낭비적인, 허비의

## bench
[béntʃ]
n. 벤치

I said, "Hoony, please sit on the bench and wait for us. Don't follow strangers."
나는 "후니, 벤치에 앉아서 우리를 기다려. 처음 보는 사람들을 따라가지 마"라고 말했어.

## stranger
[stréindʒər]
n. 처음 보는 사람, 낯선 사람

I said, "Hoony, please sit on the bench and wait for us. Don't follow strangers."
나는 "후니, 벤치에 앉아서 우리를 기다려. 처음 보는 사람들을 따라가지 마"라고 말했어.
- strange　a. 이상한, 낯선
- strangely　ad. 이상하게

## fasten
[fǽsn]
v. 매다, 죄다, 고정시키다

Then we fastened our seat belt and screamed when the ride started.
그리고 우리는 안전벨트를 매고 놀이기구가 시작되자 소리를 질렀어.
- fasten - fastened - fastened

## scream
[skríːm]
v. 소리지르다 n. 괴성

Then we fastened our seat belt and screamed when the ride started.
그리고 우리는 안전벨트를 매고 놀이기구가 시작되자 소리를 질렀어.
- scream - screamed - screamed

## missing
[mísiŋ]
a. 없어진, 행방불명인

We got off but couldn't find Hoony. He was missing.
놀이기구에서 내렸지만 후니를 찾을 수 없었어. 그가 없어진 거야.
- miss  v. 놓치다, 만나지 못하다

## mistake
[mistéik]
n. 실수

It was my mistake to leave him alone.
그를 혼자 놔둔 것은 내 실수였어.
- mistaken  a. 틀린, 오해한

## alone
[əlóun]
a. 홀로, 외로이

It was my mistake to leave him alone.
그를 혼자 놔둔 것은 내 실수였어.

## parade
[pəréid]
n. 행렬 v. 행진하다

There was a parade.
행렬이 있었어.

## follow
[fálou]
v. 따라가다

A little boy was following it.
어린 남자아이가 그것을 따라가고 있었어.
- follower  n. 수행원, 지지자
- following  a. 따르는
- follow - followed - followed

# Check Again!

**A** Translate each word or expression into Korean.

1. turn .............................
2. amusement .............................
3. stranger .............................
4. pass .............................
5. mistake .............................
6. scream .............................
7. waste .............................
8. safety .............................
9. ride .............................
10. magic .............................

**B** Translate each word or expression into English.

1. 준비가 된 .............................
2. 행렬 .............................
3. 무료의 .............................
4. 따라가다 .............................
5. 홀로, 외로이 .............................

**C** Fill in the blank with the appropriate word. Refer to the Korean.

1. F_____ your seat belt when you ride in a car.
   차를 탈 때에는 안전벨트를 매라.

2. I hate standing in a long l_____ of people inside the school cafeteria.
   나는 학교 식당에서 길게 줄 서는 것을 싫어한다.

3. My sister is m_____. I should call the police.
   내 여동생이 행방불명이다. 경찰에게 신고를 해야겠다.

4. I s_____ whenever someone tickles me.
   나는 누군가가 나에게 간지럼을 태울 때마다 소리를 지른다.

5. My h_____ is shorter than I want it to be.
   내 키는 내가 바라는 것보다 작다.

Chapter 4. Trips and Entertainment

# Chapter 4
# Trips and Entertainment

Unit 8. Hoony is at a folk village.

come to a **folk** village

go sightseeing

do a **mask** dance

have a special **dish**

# Episode

Dear Dad,

Our class is going on a field **trip**. • We came to a **folk** village. • It is a real **traditional** village. • It's like a living **museum**. • Look! There are no tall **apartment** buildings. • Most buildings here are just one-**story** tall. • Look at this colorful **roof**! • These people are doing a **mask** dance. • They are dancing with lots of **energy** like hip-hop dancers. • **Foreigners** are **gathering** to watch it. • They think it is **unique**. • Now, we are on the bus to go **sightseeing**. • We are at an **ocean** and playing beach ball games. • We played really hard and now we are **hungry**. • We are having a special **dish**. • It is **spicy** chicken. • And it is really **tasty**. • I hope to come here **again** with my **relatives**.

from Hoony

---

아빠에게,

우리 반이 견학을 가고 있어요. 우리는 민속촌에 왔어요. 정말로 전통적인 마을이에요. 그것은 살아 있는 박물관 같아요. 보세요! 높은 아파트 건물들이 하나도 없어요. 여기에 있는 대부분의 건물들은 1층 높이에요. 이 화려한 지붕을 보세요! 이 사람들은 탈춤을 추고 있어요. 그들은 힙합 댄서들처럼 활기차게 춤추고 있어요. 외국인들이 그것을 보기 위해 모여들고 있어요. 그들은 탈춤이 독특하다고 생각해요. 이제 우리는 관광을 가기 위해 버스를 탔어요. 우리는 바다에 왔고 비치볼 게임을 하고 있어요. 우리는 정말 열심히 놀아서 배가 고파요. 우리는 특별한 요리를 먹고 있어요. 매콤한 치킨이에요. 그리고 아주 맛이 있어요. 친척분들과 함께 여기 다시 오고 싶어요.

후니가

## trip
[tríp]
n. 여행

Our class is going on a field trip.
우리 반이 견학을 가고 있어요.
- go on a trip  여행을 가다

## folk
[fóuk]
a. 민속의

We came to a folk village.
우리는 민속촌에 왔어요.
- folklore  n. 민속

## traditional
[trədíʃənəl]
a. 전통의

It is a real traditional village.
정말로 전통적인 마을이에요.
- tradition  n. 전통
- traditionally  ad. 전통적으로

## museum
[mjuːzíːəm]
n. 박물관

It's like a living museum.
그것은 살아 있는 박물관 같아요.

## apartment
[əpáːrtmənt]
n. 아파트

Look! There are no tall apartment buildings.
보세요! 높은 아파트 건물들이 하나도 없어요.

## story
[stɔ́ːri]
n. 층, 이야기

Most buildings here are just one-story tall.
여기에 있는 대부분의 건물들은 1층 높이에요.

## roof
[rúːf]
n. 지붕

Look at this colorful roof!
이 화려한 지붕을 보세요!

## mask
[mǽsk]
n. 가면

These people are doing a mask dance.
이 사람들은 탈춤을 추고 있어요.

## energy
[énərdʒi]
n. 에너지, 힘

They are dancing with lots of energy like hip-hop dancers.
그들은 힙합 댄서들처럼 활기차게 춤추고 있어요.

- energetic  a. 에너지 넘치는, 활기에 찬

## foreigner
[fɔ́(ː)rinər]
n. 외국인

Foreigners are gathering to watch it.
외국인들이 그것을 보기 위해 모여들고 있어요.

- foreign  a. 외국의

## gather
[gǽðər]
v. 모이다, 더해지다

Foreigners are gathering to watch it.
외국인들이 그것을 보기 위해 모여들고 있어요.

- gather - gathered - gathered

## unique
[juːníːk]
a. 독특한

They think it is unique.
그들은 그것이 독특하다고 생각해요.

- uniqueness  n. 독특함
- uniquely  ad. 독특하게

## sightseeing
[sáitsìːiŋ]
n. 관광

Now, we are on the bus to go sightseeing.
이제 우리는 관광을 가기 위해 버스를 탔어요.

- sightsee  v. 관광하다
- go sightseeing  관광을 가다

| | |
|---|---|
| **ocean**<br>[óuʃən]<br>n. 바다 | We are at an ocean and playing beach ball games.<br>우리는 바다에 왔고 비치볼 게임을 하고 있어요. |
| **hungry**<br>[hʌ́ŋgri]<br>a. 배고픈 | We played really hard and now we are hungry.<br>우리는 정말 열심히 놀아서 배가 고파요.<br>• hunger  n. 굶주림 |
| **dish**<br>[díʃ]<br>n. 요리, 접시 | We are having a special dish.<br>우리는 특별한 요리를 먹고 있어요. |
| **spicy**<br>[spáisi]<br>a. 양념된, 매콤한 | It is spicy chicken.<br>매콤한 치킨이에요.<br>• spice  n. 양념 |
| **tasty**<br>[téisti]<br>a. 맛있는 | And it is really tasty.<br>그리고 아주 맛이 있어요.<br>• taste  v. 맛보다  n. 맛, 기호 |
| **again**<br>[əgén]<br>ad. 다시, 한 번 더 | I hope to come here again with my relatives.<br>친척분들과 함께 여기 다시 오고 싶어요. |
| **relative**<br>[rélətiv]<br>n. 친척 | I hope to come here again with my relatives.<br>친척분들과 함께 여기 다시 오고 싶어요. |

# Check Again!

**A** Translate each word or expression into Korean.

1. museum ..................
2. roof ..................
3. hungry ..................
4. sightseeing ..................
5. again ..................
6. energy ..................
7. folk ..................
8. ocean ..................
9. traditional ..................
10. relative ..................

**B** Translate each word or expression into English.

1. 모이다 ..................
2. 요리 ..................
3. 맛있는 ..................
4. 외국인 ..................
5. 가면 ..................

**C** Fill in the blank with the appropriate word. Refer to the Korean.

1. We are going on a t_____ during this summer break.
   우리는 이번 여름 방학 동안 여행을 갈 것이다.

2. Most Korean foods are s_____.
   대부분의 한국 음식들은 매콤하다.

3. They live in a two-s_____ building.
   그들은 이층 건물에서 산다.

4. This morning, they went s_____.
   오늘 아침에 그들은 관광을 갔다.

5. This picture on the wall is u_____.
   벽에 있는 이 그림은 독특하다.

Chapter 4. Trips and Entertainment

# Chapter 4
# Trips and Entertainment

Unit 9. My aunt went to India for a holiday.

**make a phone call**

go on **a package tour**

be 40 **degrees** Celsius

**have** interesting **customs**

# Episode

Dear Diary,

It was **midnight**. • Someone made a **phone call** to us. • It was **neither** my mom nor my dad. • It was my **aunt**. • She went to India for a **holiday**. • She is in New Delhi, the **capital** of India. • She went there on a **package** tour. • She met many **tourists**. • But wow, it was 40 **degrees** Celsius. • I wonder what kinds of **main** dishes and **desserts** she had. • I know that India has interesting **customs**. • For example, they use only their **right** hand at the table. • They don't use **spoons** or forks. • India **seems** to be an **interesting** country. • It doesn't **cost** a lot to travel there. • So I hope to **travel** there **someday**.

다이어리에게,
그때는 한밤중이었어. 누군가 우리에게 전화를 걸었어. 전화를 건 사람은 우리 엄마도 우리 아빠도 아니었어. 그건 바로 우리 이모였어. 이모는 휴가로 인도에 가셨어. 이모는 인도의 수도인 뉴델리에 계셔. 이모는 패키지 여행으로 거기에 가셨어. 이모는 많은 관광객들을 만났어. 그런데 와, 그곳의 기온은 40도였어. 나는 이모가 어떤 종류의 주요리와 후식을 먹었는지 궁금해. 나는 인도의 풍습들이 흥미롭다는 것을 알아. 예를 들어, 그곳 사람들은 식사 때 오른손만 사용해. 그들은 숟가락이나 포크를 사용하지 않아. 인도는 흥미로운 나라인 것 같아. 거기를 여행하는 것은 돈이 많이 들지 않아. 그래서 나는 언젠가 그곳을 여행하기를 희망해.

### midnight
[mídnàit]
n. 한밤중, 자정

It was midnight.
그때는 한밤중이었어.

---

### phone call
[fóun kɔ̀ːl]
전화를 걺, 통화

Someone made a phone call to us.
누군가 우리에게 전화를 걸었어.
- make a phone call  전화하다

---

### neither
[níːðər]
ad. ~도 아니다

It was neither my mom nor my dad.
전화를 건 사람은 우리 엄마도 우리 아빠도 아니었어.
- neither A nor B  A도 B도 아니다

---

### aunt
[ǽnt]
n. 이모, 고모, 아주머니

It was my aunt.
그건 바로 우리 이모였어.

---

### holiday
[hάlədèi]
n. 휴가, 휴일

She went to India for a holiday.
그녀는 휴가로 인도에 가셨어.
- go for a holiday  휴가차 가다

---

### capital
[kǽpitl]
n. 수도, 대문자

She is in New Delhi, the capital of India.
그녀는 인도의 수도인 뉴델리에 계셔.

## package
[pǽkidʒ]
n. 패키지, 꾸러미

She went there on a package tour.
그녀는 패키지 여행으로 거기에 가셨어.

- pack   v. 포장하다

## tourist
[túərist]
n. 관광객

She met many tourists.
그녀는 많은 관광객들을 만났어.

- tour   v. 여행하다   n. 여행

## degree
[digríː]
n. 온도

But wow, it was 40 degrees Celsius.
그런데 와, 그곳의 기온은 40도였어.

## main
[méin]
a. 주요한

I wonder what kinds of main dishes and desserts she had.
나는 그녀가 어떤 종류의 주요리와 후식을 먹었는지 궁금해.

- mainly   ad. 주로

## dessert
[dizə́ːrt]
n. 후식

I wonder what kinds of main dishes and desserts she had.
나는 그녀가 어떤 종류의 주요리와 후식을 먹었는지 궁금해.

## custom
[kʌ́stəm]
n. 풍습, 관습

I know that India has interesting customs.
나는 인도의 풍습들이 흥미롭다는 것을 알아.

## right
[ráit]
a. 오른쪽의, 옳은

For example, they use only their right hand at the table.
예를 들어, 그곳 사람들은 식사 때 오른손만 사용해.

## spoon
[spú:n]
n. 숟가락

They don't use spoons or forks.
그들은 숟가락이나 포크를 사용하지 않아.

## seem
[sí:m]
v. ~인 듯하다

India seems to be an interesting country.
인도는 흥미로운 나라인 것 같아.
- seeming  a. 외관상의
- seemly  a. 적당한  ad. 알맞게
- seem - seemed - seemed

## interesting
[íntərestiŋ]
a. 흥미있는, 재미있는

India seems to be an interesting country.
인도는 흥미로운 나라인 것 같아.
- interest  n. 흥미, 재미

## cost
[kɔ́:st]
v. 비용이 들다  n. 비용

It doesn't cost a lot to travel there.
거기를 여행하는 것은 돈이 많이 들지 않아.
- cost - cost - cost

## travel
[trǽvəl]
v. 여행하다  n. 여행

So I hope to travel there someday.
그래서 나는 언젠가 그곳을 여행하기를 희망해.
- travel - traveled - traveled

## someday
[sʌ́mdèi]
ad. 언젠가

So I hope to travel there someday.
그래서 나는 언젠가 그곳을 여행하기를 희망해.

# Check Again!

**A** Translate each word or expression into Korean.

1. travel ...................................  2. dessert ...................................

3. custom ...................................  4. seem ...................................

5. interesting ...................................  6. midnight ...................................

7. cost ...................................  8. degree ...................................

9. right ...................................  10. phone call ...................................

**B** Translate each word or expression into English.

1. 주요한 ...................................

2. 언젠가 ...................................

3. 이모 ...................................

4. 관광객 ...................................

5. 휴가, 휴일 ...................................

**C** Fill in the blank with the appropriate word. Refer to the Korean.

1. We went to Hawaii on a p_____ tour.
   우리는 패키지 여행으로 하와이에 갔다.

2. The c_____ of South Korea is Seoul.
   한국의 수도는 서울이다.

3. She enjoys eating vanilla ice cream for d_____.
   그녀는 후식으로 바닐라 아이스크림 먹는 것을 즐긴다.

4. S_____, I will show my talent to the world.
   나는 언젠가 나의 재능을 세계에 보일 것이다.

5. Brian is n_____ tall nor short.
   브라이언은 크지도 작지도 않다.

## Voca Plus!
Chapter 4. Trips and Entertainment

# On a plane

1. aisle 통로
2. window 창문
3. tray 쟁반
4. seat belt 안전벨트
5. flight attendant 승무원
6. overhead compartment 짐칸
7. headphones 헤드폰
8. armrest 팔걸이
9. passenger 승객
10. stewardess 여자 승무원
11. steward 남자 승무원

- A man is **wearing a seat belt**.
  한 남자가 안전벨트를 매고 있습니다.

- A woman is **using headphones**.
  한 여자가 헤드폰을 사용하고 있습니다.

- An old man is **asking for a drink**.
  한 나이든 남자가 음료를 부탁하고 있습니다.

- An old man is **sitting on an aisle seat**.
  한 나이든 남자가 통로 쪽에 앉아있다.

- Flight attendants are **serving passengers**.
  승무원들이 승객들의 시중을 들고 있습니다.

- A man is **taking his bag out of an overhead compartment**.
  한 남자가 짐칸에서 가방을 꺼내고 있습니다.

- There is a meal **on a tray**.
  음식은 쟁반 위에 담겨 있어요.

*Culture Plus*

### Nationality 국적

| | |
|---|---|
| + Korea 한국 | + Korean 한국인 |
| + America 미국 | + American 미국인 |
| + England 영국 | + English 영국인 |
| + China 중국 | + Chinese 중국인 |
| + Japan 일본 | + Japanese 일본인 |
| + Germany 독일 | + German 독일인 |
| + Holland 네덜란드 | + Dutch 네덜란드인 |

# STORYTELLING VOCABULARY
## GREEN

## Chapter 5. Hobbies

**Unit 10.** Welcome Danny!

**Unit 11.** It was such a long day.

**Unit 12.** Knitting doesn't suit me.

# Chapter 5
# Hobbies

## Unit 10. Welcome Danny!

**do** someone **a favor**

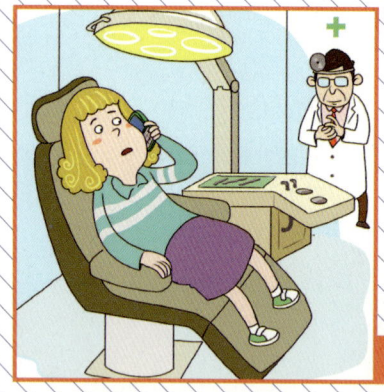

**have an appointment** with a dentist

**have a sign saying** Danny

**hold** a lollipop

# Episode

Sara: Hello? Bomi, can you do me a **favor**? • Could you go to the **airport**? • I have an **appointment** with a dentist. • Would you **pick** up my **cousin** for me?

Bomi: Sure.

Sara said Danny **grew** up in the US. • The airport is **huge** and it's **crowded**. • I have a **sign** saying Danny. • I'm **curious** what he looks like. • Sara said that he is **handsome**. • I **wonder** about his **appearance**. • How should I **welcome** Danny? • Should I kiss him on the **cheek**? • **Finally**, I see a good-looking man. • But a boy with **curly** hair is walking **towards** me. • He is **holding** a lollipop. • That's Danny!

---

사라: 여보세요? 보미, 부탁 들어줄 수 있니? 공항에 가줄 수 있어? 나는 치과에 예약이 돼 있어. 나를 위해 내 사촌을 데리러 가줄 수 있어?

보미: 그래.

사라는 대니가 미국에서 자랐다고 말했다. 공항은 크고 혼잡하다. 나는 대니라고 써진 표지판을 가지고 있다. 나는 대니가 어떻게 생겼을까 궁금하다. 사라는 그가 잘생겼다고 말했다. 나는 그의 외모가 궁금하다. 대니를 어떻게 환영해야 할까? 볼에다 뽀뽀를 해야 할까? 마침내 잘생긴 남자가 보인다. 하지만 곱슬 머리의 남자아이가 나를 향해 걸어오고 있다. 그 애는 막대 사탕을 들고 있다. 그 애가 바로 대니야.

## favor
[féivər]
n. 부탁, 호의
v. 호의를 보이다, 찬성하다

Hello? Bomi, can you do me a favor?
여보세요? 보미, 부탁 들어줄 수 있어?

- favorable  a. 호의적인, 유리한
- do a favor  부탁을 들어주다

## airport
[ɛ́ərpɔ̀ːrt]
n. 공항

Could you go to the airport?
공항에 가줄 수 있어?

## appointment
[əpɔ́intmənt]
n. 약속, 예약

I have an appointment with a dentist.
나는 치과에 예약이 돼 있어.

- appoint  v. 정하다, 약속하다
- make an appointment  약속을 잡다
- have an appointment  약속이 있다
- confirm an appointment  약속을 확인하다

## pick
[pík]
v. 잡다, 고르다

Would you pick up my cousin for me?
나를 위해 내 사촌을 데리러 가줄 수 있어?

- pick up  마중나가다, 데리러 가다
- pick - picked - picked

## cousin
[kʌ́zn]
n. 사촌

Would you pick up my cousin for me?
나를 위해 내 사촌을 데리러 가줄 수 있어?

## grow
[gróu]
v. 자라다

Sara said Danny grew up in the US.
사라는 대니가 미국에서 자랐다고 말했다.

- growth  n. 성장
- grow up  성장하다, 자라다
- grow - grew - grown

## huge
[hjúːdʒ]
a. 커다란

The airport is huge and it's crowded.
공항은 크고 혼잡하다.

## crowded
[kráudid]
a. 혼잡한, 붐비는

The airport is huge and it's crowded.
공항은 크고 혼잡하다.
- crowd　n. 무리, 군중

## sign
[sáin]
n. 표지, 신호　v. 서명하다

I have a sign saying Danny.
나는 대니라고 써진 표지판을 가지고 있다.

## curious
[kjúəriəs]
a. 알고 싶어하는, 호기심이 강한

I'm curious what he looks like.
나는 대니가 어떻게 생겼을까 궁금하다.
- curiosity　n. 호기심

## handsome
[hǽnsəm]
a. 잘생긴

Sara said that he is handsome.
사라는 그가 잘생겼다고 말했다.

## wonder
[wʌ́ndər]
v. 궁금해 하다
n. 경이, 기적

I wonder about his appearance.
나는 그의 외모가 궁금하다.
- wonderful　a. 놀랄 만한, 경이적인
- wonder - wondered - wondered

## appearance
[əpíərəns]
n. 외모

I wonder about his appearance.
나는 그의 외모가 궁금하다.
- appear　v. 나타나다, ~인 듯하다

## welcome
[wélkəm]
v. 환영하다  n. 환영

How should I welcome Danny?
대니를 어떻게 환영해야 할까?
- welcome - welcomed - welcomed

## cheek
[tʃíːk]
n. 볼

Should I kiss him on the cheek?
볼에다 뽀뽀를 해야 할까?

## finally
[fáinəli]
ad. 드디어

Finally, I see a good-looking man.
마침내 잘생긴 남자가 보인다.
- final  a. 마지막의

## curly
[kə́ːrli]
a. 곱슬 머리의

But a boy with curly hair is walking towards me.
하지만 곱슬 머리의 남자아이가 나를 향해 걸어오고 있다.
- curl  v. 꼬다, 곱슬곱슬하게 하다

## towards
[təwɔ́ːrdz]
ad. ~을 향하여

But a boy with curly hair is walking towards me.
하지만 곱슬 머리의 남자아이가 나를 향해 걸어오고 있다.

## hold
[hóuld]
v. 들다, 쥐다

He is holding a lollipop.
그는 막대 사탕을 들고 있다.
- hold - held - held

# Check Again!

**A** Translate each word or expression into Korean.

1. welcome .............................
2. handsome .............................
3. favor .............................
4. huge .............................
5. pick up .............................
6. appointment .............................
7. grow up .............................
8. crowded .............................
9. towards .............................
10. hold .............................

**B** Translate each word or expression into English.

1. 사촌 .............................
2. 표지 .............................
3. 공항 .............................
4. 궁금해 하다 .............................
5. 알고 싶어하는 .............................

**C** Fill in the blank with the appropriate word. Refer to the Korean.

1. The guy gave me a kiss on the c_____ .
   그 남자는 나의 볼에 뽀뽀를 했다.

2. He could f_____ run 100m in 13 seconds.
   그는 드디어 100미터를 13초에 뛸 수 있었다.

3. My hair gets c_____ when it rains.
   나의 머리카락은 비가 올 때 곱슬거린다.

4. Could you do me a f_____ ?
   너는 나의 부탁을 들어줄 수 있니?

5. A_____ is too important these days.
   오늘날 외모는 너무 중요하다.

# Chapter 5
# Hobbies

Unit 11. It was such a long day.

**be able to read** Korean

put up **a national flag**

give a **boost**

**walk along** the bike path

# Episode

Danny: Is today a **national** holiday?
Sara: Yes.
Danny: Why do people put up national **flags**?
Sara: It's **common** in Korea. • It's the **way** we **show** our **respect** to our nation.
Danny: I see. • Oh, I'm **able** to read some Korean. • But how do you **pronounce** crabs and dogs in Korean?
Sara: They are kind of **similar**. • Danny, come here. • You should walk on the **sidewalk**.

Danny wanted to throw a ball into the **basketball** hoop. • He asked us to give him a **boost**. • He was **repeatedly** asking us to do it. • He asked us to do it more than 10 **times**. • He also **required** us to do **millions** of other things. • Danny wanted to **ride** a tricycle. • We had to walk **along** the bike **path**, following him. • He also asked us, "Who is more **powerful**, Batman or Superman?" • At the end of the day, we were **nearly** dead. • We needed **rest**. • It was such a long day.

대니: 오늘이 국경일이에요?
사라: 응.
대니: 왜 사람들은 국기를 다는 거죠?
사라: 그것은 한국에서 흔한 일이야. 우리나라에 대한 존경심을 나타내는 방법이야.
대니: 이제 알겠네요. 참, 나는 한국어를 좀 읽을 수 있어요. 한국말로 게와 개를 어떻게 발음해요?
사라: 둘은 조금 비슷해. 대니, 이리 와. 인도로 걸어야 해.

대니는 농구링에 골을 던지고 싶어했다. 대니는 우리에게 자기를 밀어 올려 달라고 부탁했다. 우리에게 그것을 해달라고 반복해서 부탁했다. 대니는 우리에게 10번 이상 그것을 해달라고 부탁했다. 또한 우리에게 수많은 다른 일을 할 것을 요구했다. 대니는 세발 자전거를 타고 싶어했다. 우리는 자전거 도로를 따라 걸으면서 대니를 따라가야만 했다. 그는 또한 배트맨과 슈퍼맨 중 누가 더 힘이 센지 우리에게 질문했다. 하루가 끝날 무렵 우리는 거의 죽을 지경이었다. 우리는 휴식이 필요했다. 정말 긴 하루였다.

## national
[næʃənəl]
a. 국가의

Is today a national holiday?
오늘이 국경일이에요?
- nation   n. 국가

## flag
[flæg]
n. 깃발

Why do people put up national flags?
왜 사람들은 국기를 다는 거죠?

## common
[kɔ́mən]
a. 흔한

It's common in Korea.
그것은 한국에서 흔한 일이야.

## way
[wéi]
n. 방법, 길

It's the way we show our respect to our nation.
우리나라에 대한 존경심을 나타내는 방법이야.

## show
[ʃóu]
v. 보여주다, 나타내다

It's the way we show our respect to our nation. 우리나라에 대한 존경심을 나타내는 방법이야.
- show - showed - showed

## respect
[rispékt]
n. 존경, 존중   v. 존경하다

It's the way we show our respect to our nation.
우리나라에 대한 존경심을 나타내는 방법이야.
- respectable   a. 존경할 만한
- respectful   a. 공손한, 정중한

## able
[éibəl]
a. ~할 수 있는

Oh, I'm able to read some Korean.
참, 나는 한국어를 좀 읽을 수 있어요.
- ability   n. 능력
- be able to   ~할 수 있다

## pronounce
[prənáuns]
v. 발음하다

But how do you pronounce crabs and dogs in Korean?
그런데 한국말로 게와 개를 어떻게 발음해요?
- pronunciation   n. 발음
- pronounce - pronounced - pronounced

## similar
[símələr]
a. 비슷한, 유사한

They are kind of similar.
둘은 조금 비슷해.
- similarity  n. 유사, 비슷함
- similarly  ad. 비슷하게

## sidewalk
[sáidwɔ̀:k]
n. 인도

Danny, come here. You should walk on the sidewalk.
대니, 이리 와. 인도로 걸어야 해.

## basketball
[bǽskitbɔ̀:l]
n. 농구

Danny wanted to throw a ball into the basketball hoop.
대니는 농구링에 골을 던지고 싶어했다.

## boost
[bú:st]
n. 밀어 올리기  v. 밀어 올리다

He asked us to give him a boost.
그는 우리에게 자기를 들어 올려 달라고 부탁했다.
- give a boost  들어 올리다

## repeatedly
[ripí:tidli]
ad. 되풀이하여

He was repeatedly asking us to do it.
그는 우리에게 그것을 해달라고 반복해서 부탁했다.
- repeat  v. 반복하다, 되풀이하다
- repetition  n. 반복  · repetitive  a. 반복적인

## time
[táim]
n. ~번, ~배

He asked us to do it more than 10 times.
그는 우리에게 10번 이상 그것을 해달라고 부탁했다.

## require
[rikwáiər]
v. 요구하다

He also required us to do millions of other things.
그는 또한 우리에게 수많은 다른 일을 할 것을 요구했다.
- requirement  n. 요구
- require - required - required

## million
[míljən]
n. 백만

He also required us to do millions of other things.
그는 또한 우리에게 수많은 다른 일을 할 것을 요구했다.
- millions of  a. 수많은

## ride
[ráid]
v. 타다 n. 탐, 탈것

Danny wanted to ride a tricycle.
대니는 세발 자전거를 타고 싶어했다.
- ride - rode - ridden

## along
[əlɔ́ːŋ]
prep. ~을 따라서

We had to walk along the bike path, following him.
우리는 자전거 도로를 따라 걸으면서 그를 따라가야만 했다.

## path
[pǽθ]
n. 길, 도로

We had to walk along the bike path, following him.
우리는 자전거 도로를 따라 걸으면서 그를 따라가야만 했다.

## powerful
[páuərfəl]
a. 강한

He also asked us, "Who is more powerful, Batman or Superman?"
그는 또한 배트맨과 슈퍼맨 중 누가 더 힘이 센지 우리에게 질문했다.
- power  n. 힘

## nearly
[níərli]
ad. 거의

At the end of the day, we were nearly dead.
하루가 끝날 무렵 우리는 거의 죽을 지경이었다.
- near  a. 가까운

## rest
[rést]
n. 휴식 v. 쉬다

We needed rest.
우리는 휴식이 필요했다.

# Check Again!

**A** Translate each word or expression into Korean.

1. million ......................
2. respect ......................
3. require ......................
4. along ......................
5. ride ......................
6. powerful ......................
7. similar ......................
8. show ......................
9. path ......................
10. time ......................

**B** Translate each word or expression into English.

1. 흔한 ......................
2. 되풀이하여 ......................
3. 휴식 ......................
4. 국가의 ......................
5. 발음하다 ......................

**C** Fill in the blank with the appropriate word. Refer to the Korean.

1. Please give me a b_____. I can't reach it.
   나를 들어 올려줘. 손이 안 닿잖아.

2. The b_____ player threw the ball into the hoop.
   그 농구 선수는 공을 링 안으로 던졌다.

3. The twins were a_____ to play the violin very well.
   그 쌍둥이는 바이올린을 매우 잘 연주할 수 있었다.

4. What side of the s_____ should I walk on?
   나는 인도의 어느 쪽에서 걸어야 하죠?

5. The truck n_____ bumped into the tree.
   트럭이 거의 나무를 칠 뻔했다.

# Chapter 5
# Hobbies

Unit 12. Knitting doesn't suit me.

**celebrate** the 22nd day

**act** more **like** a girl

**fail to** finish

# Episode

Dear Diary,

Sara has a new boyfriend. • We **celebrated** their 22nd day **together** last week. • I **arranged** the celebration party. • Sara got a **present**.

Sara: Hello? Thanks for **host**ing the party.
Bomi: What's the **matter** with me, Sara? • I can't be **warm** without a boyfriend this winter.
Sara: Why don't you **act** more like a girl? • **Change** your hobbies **around**. • **Knitting** might be good.
Bomi: Hmm… I **remember** seeing other girls knit. • What are some of the **basic** items I can knit?
Sara: **Socks** or a scarf is OK.

I **decided** to try knitting a scarf. • But I **failed** to finish it. • My fingers were **aching**.
Sara, I'm not as **patient** as you are. • Knitting doesn't **suit** me. • I should just try to **be myself**.

---

다이어리에게,
사라는 새로운 남자친구가 있어. 우리는 지난주에 함께 두 사람의 22일을 축하했어. 나는 축하 파티를 준비했어. 사라는 선물을 받았어.

사라: 여보세요? 파티를 주최해 줘서 고마워.
보미: 사라, 나는 뭐가 문제일까? 이번 겨울은 남자친구 없으면 따뜻하지 못할 거야.
사라: 좀 더 여성스럽게 행동하는 건 어때? 취미를 바꿔 봐. 뜨개질도 괜찮아.
보미: 흠… 내 기억에 몇몇 여자아이들이 뜨개질하는 것을 본 것 같아. 내가 뜨개질할 수 있는 기본적인 아이템은 뭐야?
사라: 양말이나 목도리가 괜찮아.

나는 목도리를 뜨기로 결정했어. 하지만 완성하지는 못했어. 손가락이 너무 아팠어.
사라, 나는 너만큼 참을성이 있지 않아. 뜨개질은 나와 어울리지 않아. 나는 나에게 어울리게 행동하는 편이 낫겠어.

## celebrate
[séləbrèit]
v. 축하하다

We celebrated their 22nd day last week together.
우리는 지난주에 함께 그들의 22일을 축하했어.

- celebration   n. 축하
- celebrate - celebrated - celebrated

## together
[təgéðər]
ad. 함께, 같이

We celebrated their 22nd day last week together.
우리는 지난주에 함께 그들의 22일을 축하했어.

## arrange
[əréindʒ]
v. 준비하다

I arranged the celebration party.
나는 축하 파티를 준비했어.

- arrangement   n. 준비
- arrange - arranged - arranged

## present
[prézənt]
n. 선물  a. ~에 출석한
v. 증정하다, 제출하다

Sara got a present.
사라는 선물을 받았어.

## host
[hóust]
v. 주최하다  n. 주최자

Hello? Thanks for hosting the party.
여보세요? 파티를 주최해 줘서 고마워.

- host - hosted - hosted

## matter
[mǽtər]
n. 문제  v. 문제가 되다

What's the matter with me, Sara?
사라, 나는 뭐가 문제일까?

## warm
[wɔ́ːrm]
a. 따뜻한

I can't be warm without a boyfriend this winter.
이번 겨울은 남자친구 없으면 따뜻하지 못할 거야.

- warmth   n. 따뜻함

## act
[ǽkt]
v. 행동하다

Why don't you act more like a girl?
좀 더 여성스럽게 행동하는 건 어때?
- action  n. 행동, 연기
- act - acted - acted

## change
[tʃéindʒ]
v. 바꾸다  n. 변화

Change your hobbies around.
취미를 바꿔 봐.
- changeable  a. 변하기 쉬운, 변덕스러운
- change - changed - changed

## around
[əráund]
ad. 주위에, 근처에

Change your hobbies around.
취미를 바꿔 봐.

## knitting
[nítiŋ]
n. 뜨개질

Knitting might be good.
뜨개질도 괜찮아.
- knit  v. 뜨개질하다

## remember
[rimémbər]
v. 기억하다

Hmm... I remember seeing other girls knit.
흠… 내 기억에 몇몇 여자아이들이 뜨개질하는 것을 본 것 같아.
- remembrance  n. 기억
- remember - remembered - remembered

## basic
[béisik]
a. 기초의, 근본의

What are some of the basic items I can knit?
내가 뜨개질할 수 있는 기본적인 아이템은 뭐야?
- basics  n. 기본  • basically  ad. 근본적으로

## socks
[sáks]
n. 양말

Socks or a scarf is OK.
양말이나 목도리가 괜찮아.

## decide
[disáid]
v. 결정하다

I decided to try knitting a scarf.
나는 목도리를 뜨기로 결정했어.
- decision  n. 결정
- decide - decided - decided

## fail
[féil]
v. 실패하다

But I failed to finish it.
하지만 완성하지는 못했어.
- failure  n. 실패
- fail to + V  ~하는 것을 실패하다
- fail - failed - failed

## ache
[éik]
v. 아프다  n. 통증

My fingers were aching.
손가락이 너무 아팠어.
- ache - ached - ached

## patient
[péiʃənt]
a. 참을성 있는

Sara, I'm not as patient as you are.
사라, 나는 너만큼 참을성이 있지 않아.
- patience  n. 참을성, 인내
- impatient  a. 참을성이 없는

## suit
[súːt]
v. 어울리다, 적당하다

Knitting doesn't suit me.
뜨개질은 나와 어울리지 않아.
- suitable  a. 적당한
- suit - suited - suited

## be oneself
[bi wʌnsélf]
자연스럽게 행동하다,
자기 자신을 잃지 않다

I should just try to be myself.
나는 나에게 어울리게 행동하는 편이 낫겠어.

# Check Again!

**A** Translate each word or expression into Korean.

1. basic ........................
2. together ........................
3. matter ........................
4. act ........................
5. present ........................
6. be oneself ........................
7. warm ........................
8. arrange ........................
9. ache ........................
10. patient ........................

**B** Translate each word or expression into English.

1. 바꾸다 ........................
2. 주위에, 근처에 ........................
3. 뜨개질 ........................
4. 주최하다 ........................
5. 결정하다 ........................

**C** Fill in the blank with the appropriate word. Refer to the Korean.

1. I can't r_____ where I left my bag.
   나는 내 가방을 어디에 두었는지 기억이 안 난다.

2. The girl f_____ to find her bag.
   그 여자아이는 자기 가방을 찾지 못했다.

3. Blue clothes s_____ me better than green clothes.
   파란색 옷은 초록색 옷보다 나에게 더 어울려요.

4. I would like to c_____ your graduation.
   나는 너의 졸업을 축하해 주고 싶어.

5. You are not as p_____ as your younger sister.
   너는 네 여동생만큼 참을성이 있지는 않구나.

Chapter 5. Hobbies  **97**

# Voca Plus!

Chapter 5. Hobbies

## In a baseball park

1. baseball park 야구장
2. bat 배트
3. glove/mitt 글러브
4. baseball diamond 내야, 야구장
5. pitcher 투수
6. catcher 포수
7. first base 1루
8. second base 2루
9. third base 3루
10. dugout 더그아웃 (선수 대기소)
11. bullpen 불펜 (구원 투수 연습장)
12. home plate 본루, 홈 베이스
13. umpire 심판

- The players are **in** the baseball park.
  선수들이 야구장에 있다.

- The umpire is **behind** the catcher.
  심판은 포수 뒤에 있다.

- The catcher is **in front of** the umpire.
  포수는 심판 앞에 있다.

- Some players are practicing **in** the bullpen.
  어떤 선수들은 불펜에서 연습을 하고 있다.

- A player is running **towards** the second base.
  한 선수가 2루를 향해 뛰어 가고 있다.

- The batter is standing **near** the home plate.
  타자는 홈 플레이트 근처에 서 있다.

- Some players are cheering for their team **in** the dugout.
  어떤 선수들은 더그아웃에서 그들 팀을 응원하고 있다.

## Culture Plus

### Hobbies 취미

- mountain climbing 등산
- windsurfing 윈드 서핑
- horseback riding 승마
- bowling 볼링
- aerobics 에어로빅
- jogging 조깅
- swimming 수영
- scuba diving 스쿠버 다이빙
- skating 스케이팅
- skiing 스키
- roller skating 롤러 스케이팅
- dancing 댄스
- knitting 뜨개질
- yachting 요트타기

# STORYTELLING VOCABULARY

GREEN

## Chapter 6. Health

**Unit 13.** I had the mumps.

**Unit 14.** I want fried chicken.

# Chapter 6
# Health

## Unit 13. I had the mumps.

**look into** the mirror

**look like** a monster

**go to** a clinic

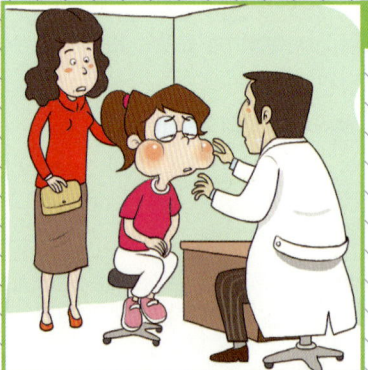

**return to** beauty

# Episode

Dear Diary,

I was **absent** from school today. • I started to have a **fever** last night. • I also had a **sore** throat. • It **hurt** me a lot. • My **voice sounded** strange, too. • I said to myself, "Do I just have the **flu**? • Or do I have a serious **disease**?" • Early this morning, I looked into the bathroom **mirror**. • I asked, 'who are you?' to my **reflection**. • I looked like I had **candy** in both cheeks. • Hoony and Seri said, "Hey, you look like a **monster**!" • I went to a **clinic** with my mom. • The doctor **examined** me and said I had the **mumps**. • She told me to take **medicine**. • Then I would **recover** soon. • Like Princess Fiona, I will return to **beauty**. • Tomorrow I have an **exam**. • Luckily, Princess Fiona can relax in an **armchair** at home!

다이어리에게,

나는 오늘 학교에 결석했어. 어젯밤에 열이 나기 시작했어. 나는 목도 아팠어. 정말 많이 아팠어. 목소리도 이상했어. 나는 "단지 독감이 걸린 거야? 아니면 심각한 병에 걸린 거야?"라고 혼잣말을 했어. 오늘 아침 일찍 화장실 거울을 보았어. 나는 '너는 누구야?'라고 거울에 비친 내 모습에게 물었어. 나는 양쪽 볼에 사탕을 물고 있는 것처럼 보였어. 후니와 세리는 "이봐, 언니(누나)는 괴물처럼 보여!"라고 말했어. 나는 엄마와 함께 병원에 갔어. 의사 선생님은 나를 진찰하고 내가 볼거리에 걸렸다고 하셨어. 나에게 약을 먹으라고 하셨어. 그러면 나는 곧 회복할 거야. 피오나 공주처럼 나는 다시 아름다워질 거야. 내일 나는 시험이 있어. 운이 좋게도 피오나 공주는 집에서 안락의자에 앉아 쉴 수 있어!

## absent
[ǽbsənt]
a. 결석한  v. 결석하다

I was absent from school today.
나는 오늘 학교에 결석했어.
- absence  n. 결석

## fever
[fíːvər]
n. 열

I started to have a fever last night.
나는 어젯밤에 열이 나기 시작했어.
- feverish  a. 열이 있는

## sore
[sɔ́ːr]
a. 아픈

I also had a sore throat.
나는 목도 아팠어.
- soreness  n. 아픔

## hurt
[hə́ːrt]
v. 아프게 하다  n. 상처, 고통

It hurt me a lot.
정말 많이 아팠어.
- hurtful  a. 고통을 주는, 해로운
- hurt - hurt - hurt

## voice
[vɔ́is]
n. 목소리, 음성

My voice sounded strange, too.
목소리도 이상했어.

## sound
[sáund]
v. ~하게 들리다  n. 소리

My voice sounded strange, too.
목소리도 이상했어.
- sound - sounded - sounded

## flu
[flúː]
n. 독감

I said to myself, "Do I just have the flu? Or do I have a serious disease?"
나는 "단지 독감이 걸린 거야? 아니면 심각한 병에 걸린 거야?"라고 혼잣말을 했어.

## disease
[dizíːz]
n. 질병

I said to myself, "Do I just have the flu? Or do I have a serious disease?"
나는 "단지 독감이 걸린 거야? 아니면 심각한 병에 걸린 거야?"라고 혼잣말을 했어.

## mirror
[mírər]
n. 거울

Early this morning, I looked into the bathroom mirror.
오늘 아침 일찍 나는 화장실 거울을 보았어.

## reflection
[riflékʃən]
n. 반영, 반사

I asked, 'who are you?' to my reflection.
나는 '너는 누구야?'라고 거울에 비친 내 모습에게 물었어.

- **reflect** v. 반영하다
- **reflective** a. 반영하는, 반사하는

## candy
[kǽndi]
n. 사탕

I looked like I had candy in both cheeks.
나는 양쪽 볼에 사탕을 물고 있는 것처럼 보였어.

## monster
[mánstər]
n. 괴물

Hoony and Seri said, "Hey, you look like a monster!"
후니와 세리는 "이봐, 괴물처럼 보여!"라고 말했어.

## clinic
[klínik]
n. 병원, 진료소

I went to a clinic with my mom.
나는 엄마와 함께 병원에 갔어.

## examine
[igzǽmin]
v. 진찰하다

The doctor **examined** me and said I had the mumps.
의사 선생님은 나를 진찰하고 내가 볼거리에 걸렸다고 하셨어.
- examination   n. 진찰, 검사, 시험
- examine - examined - examined

## mumps
[mʌmps]
n. 볼거리, 유행성 이하선염

The doctor examined me and said I had the **mumps**.
의사 선생님은 나를 진찰하고 내가 볼거리에 걸렸다고 하셨어.

## medicine
[médəsən]
n. 약

She told me to take **medicine**.
그녀는 나에게 약을 먹으라고 하셨어.
- medical   a. 의학의
- take medicine   약을 먹다

## recover
[rikʌ́vər]
v. 회복하다

Then I would **recover** soon.
그러면 나는 곧 회복할 거야.
- recovery   n. 회복
- recover - recovered - recovered

## beauty
[bjúːti]
n. 아름다움, 미인

Like Princess Fiona, I will return to **beauty**.
피오나 공주처럼 나는 다시 아름다워질 거야.
- beautiful   a. 아름다운

## exam
[igzǽm]
n. 시험

Tomorrow I have an **exam**.
내일 나는 시험이 있어.

## armchair
[ɑ́ːrmtʃɛ̀ər]
n. 안락의자

Luckily, Princess Fiona can relax in an **armchair** at home!
운이 좋게도 피오나 공주는 집에서 안락의자에 앉아 쉴 수 있어!

# Check Again!

**A** Translate each word or expression into Korean.

1. armchair .................................
2. absent .................................
3. disease .................................
4. examine .................................
5. mirror .................................
6. flu .................................
7. sound .................................
8. reflection .................................
9. beauty .................................
10. voice .................................

**B** Translate each word or expression into English.

1. 아프게 하다 .................................
2. 회복하다 .................................
3. 열 .................................
4. 병원 .................................
5. 괴물 .................................

**C** Fill in the blank with the appropriate word. Refer to the Korean.

1. Sujin was a _____ from school because she was sick.
   수진이는 아파서 오늘 학교에 결석했다.

2. I don't like my r_____ in the mirror.
   나는 거울에 비친 나의 모습이 마음에 안 든다.

3. I wish I were sick so I wouldn't need to take the e_____ tomorrow.
   나는 내일 시험을 볼 필요가 없게 아팠으면 좋겠다.

4. He took a cough m_____.
   그는 기침약을 먹었다.

5. Ouch! You stepped on my hands. My hands are s_____.
   아야, 네가 내 손을 밟았어. 내 손이 너무 아파.

Chapter 6. Health  **107**

# Chapter 6
# Health

## Unit 14. I want fried chicken.

be not **healthy**

**look in** the refrigerator

**have** some skin **problems**

**have no choice**

# Episode

Mom: Bomi, no more **fast food**!

Bomi: Look in the **refrigerator**, mom. • There's no coke, no ham, no **fried** chicken. • There are only **vegetables**. • Mom, I want **meat**.

Mom: Those foods are not **healthy**.

Bomi: Mom, I'm **starving**.

Mom: There are **potatoes** in the rice **cooker**. • And don't forget to **chew** at least 30 times before you **swallow** your food.

I have some **skin** problems. • It gets **worse** in winter. • Mom read in a **magazine** that I need a special **diet**. • Mom went to the **bakery**. • She bought **whole grain** bread. • It doesn't look **appetizing** at all. • I **need soft** cheesecake. • Mom, don't I have any **choice**?

---

엄마: 보미, 더 이상 패스트푸드 먹으면 안 돼!
보미: 냉장고 안을 봐요, 엄마. 콜라도, 햄도, 튀긴 치킨도 없어요. 야채뿐이잖아요. 엄마, 전 고기를 원해요.
엄마: 그 음식들은 건강에 좋지 않아.
보미: 엄마, 정말 배고파요.
엄마: 밥솥에 감자 있어. 삼키기 전에 음식물을 30회 이상 씹는 것을 잊지 마라.

나는 피부 질환이 있다. 겨울에는 더 심해진다. 엄마는 잡지에서 내가 특별한 식이요법이 필요하다는 것을 읽으셨다. 엄마는 빵집에 가셨다. 엄마는 통밀빵을 사왔다. 그것은 전혀 맛있어 보이지 않는다. 나는 부드러운 치즈케익이 필요하다. 엄마, 나에게는 선택권이 없는 건가요?

## fast food
[fǽst fúːd]
패스트푸드

Bomi, no more fast food!
보미, 더 이상 패스트푸드 먹으면 안 돼!

## refrigerator
[rifrìdʒəréitər]
n. 냉장고

Look in the refrigerator, mom.
냉장고 안을 봐요, 엄마.
- refrigerate   v. 냉장 보관하다

## fried
[fráid]
a. 튀긴

There's no coke, no ham, no fried chicken.
콜라도, 햄도, 튀긴 치킨도 없어요.
- fry   v. 튀기다

## vegetable
[védʒətəbəl]
n. 야채

There are only vegetables.
야채뿐이에요.

## meat
[míːt]
n. 육류

Mom, I want meat.
엄마, 전 고기를 원해요.

## healthy
[hélθi]
a. 건강에 좋은, 건강한

Those foods are not healthy.
그 음식들은 건강에 좋지 않아.
- health   n. 건강

## starving
[stáːrviŋ]
a. 배고픈

Mom, I'm starving.
엄마, 저 정말 배고파요.
- starve   v. 굶주리다
- starvation   n. 굶주림, 기아

## potato
[pətéitou]
n. 감자

There are potatoes in the rice cooker.
밥솥에 감자 있어.

## cooker
[kúkər]
n. 요리기구

There are potatoes in the rice cooker.
밥솥에 감자 있어.

- cook  v. 요리하다  n. 요리사

## chew
[tʃúː]
v. 씹다

And don't forget to chew at least 30 times before you swallow your food.
삼키기 전에 음식물을 30회 이상 씹는 것을 잊지 마라.

- chew - chewed - chewed

## swallow
[swálou]
v. 삼키다

And don't forget to chew at least 30 times before you swallow your food.
삼키기 전에 음식물을 30회 이상 씹는 것을 잊지 마라.

- swallow - swallowed - swallowed

## skin
[skín]
n. 피부

I have some skin problems.
나는 피부 질환이 있다.

- skinny  a. 깡마른

## worse
[wə́ːrs]
a. 더 나쁜

It gets worse in winter.
겨울에는 더 심해진다.

- worst  a. 가장 나쁜

## magazine
[mǽgəzíːn]
n. 잡지

Mom read in a magazine that I need a special diet.
엄마는 잡지에서 내가 특별한 식이요법이 필요하다는 것을 읽으셨다.

Chapter 6. Health

## diet
[dáiət]
n. 식이요법
v. 식이요법을 하다

Mom read in a magazine that I need a special diet.
엄마는 잡지에서 내가 특별한 식이요법이 필요하다는 것을 읽으셨다.

## bakery
[béikəri]
n. 빵집, 제과점

Mom went to the bakery.
엄마는 빵집에 가셨다.
- bake  v. 굽다

## whole
[hóul]
a. 온전한, 전체의, 있는 그대로의

She bought whole grain bread.
통밀빵을 사왔다.

## grain
[gréin]
n. 곡물

She bought whole grain bread.
통밀빵을 사왔다.

## appetizing
[ǽpitàiziŋ]
a. 식욕을 돋우는

It doesn't look appetizing at all.
그것은 전혀 맛있어 보이지 않는다.
- appetite  n. 식욕

## need
[ní:d]
v. 필요하다  n. 필요

I need soft cheesecake.
나는 부드러운 치즈케익이 필요하다.
- needful  a. 필요한  • needy  a. 가난한
- need - needed - needed

## soft
[sɔ́(:)ft]
a. 부드러운

I need soft cheesecake.
나는 부드러운 치즈케익이 필요하다.
- softness  n. 부드러움

## choice
[tʃɔ́is]
n. 선택(권)

Mom, don't I have any choice?
엄마, 나에게는 선택권이 없는 건가요?
- choose  v. 고르다

# Check Again!

**A** Translate each word or expression into Korean.

1. appetizing ..............................
2. diet ..............................
3. starving ..............................
4. skin ..............................
5. meat ..............................
6. refrigerator ..............................
7. worse ..............................
8. soft ..............................
9. chew ..............................
10. choice ..............................

**B** Translate each word or expression into English.

1. 필요하다 ..............................
2. 요리기구 ..............................
3. 삼키다 ..............................
4. 건강에 좋은 ..............................
5. 온전한 ..............................

**C** Fill in the blank with the appropriate word. Refer to the Korean.

1. I don't want to go there, but I have no c_____.
   나는 거기에 가고 싶지 않지만 선택의 여지가 없어.

2. Bread tastes best when it is baked at a b_____.
   빵은 빵집에서 구웠을 때 가장 맛있다.

3. The children on TV are s_____.
   TV에 나온 아이들이 굶주리고 있다.

4. These m_____ are filled with stylish people.
   이 잡지들은 멋스러운 사람들로 가득 차 있다.

5. I like v_____ salad.
   나는 야채 샐러드를 좋아해.

Chapter 6. Health   113

Chapter 6. Health

# My body

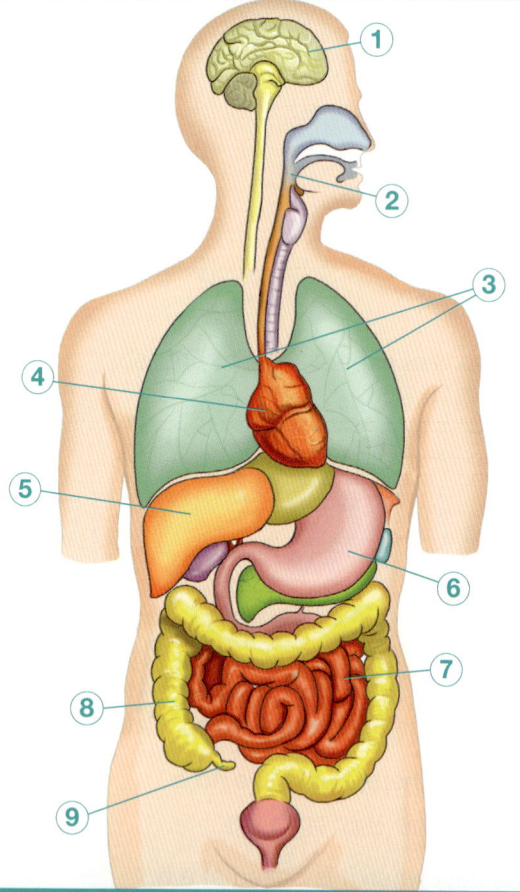

1. brain 뇌
2. throat 목구멍
3. lungs 허파(복수형)
4. heart 심장
5. liver 간
6. stomach 위
7. small intestine 소장
8. large intestine 대장
9. appendix 충수

✚ My **brain** enables me to think.
나의 뇌는 내가 생각할 수 있게 해요.

✚ My **heart** pumps blood through the body.
나의 심장은 온몸 전체로 혈액을 펌프질 해요.

✚ My **lungs** enable me to breathe.
나의 폐는 호흡할 수 있게 해요.

✚ My **stomach** digests food.
나의 위는 음식을 소화시켜요.

✚ My **intestines** help nutrients to move.
나의 장은 음식물이 움직이도록 해요.

## Culture Plus

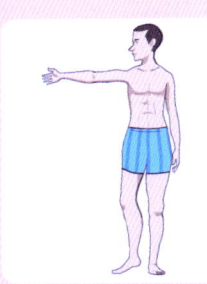

**Our body** 신체

| | |
|---|---|
| ✚head 머리 | ✚waist 허리 |
| ✚face 얼굴 | ✚thigh 허벅지 |
| ✚neck 목 | ✚knee 무릎 |
| ✚shoulder 어깨 | ✚leg 다리 |
| ✚chest 가슴 | ✚calf 종아리 |
| ✚elbow 팔꿈치 | ✚ankle 발목 |
| ✚wrist 손목 | ✚foot (단수형) cf) feet 발(복수형) |

# STORYTELLING VOCABULARY

GREEN

## Chapter 7. People

**Unit 15.** Our teacher became an April Fool.

**Unit 16.** Dad, don't forget your New Year's resolutions.

**Unit 17.** I envy Sujin's aunt.

**Unit 18.** I remember the first day we met.

# Chapter 7
# People

Unit 15. Our teacher became an April Fool.

**run out** the door

**rub** the floor **hard**

**lose one's balance** and slip

smile and stop one's **tricks**

# Episode

Dear Diary,

It was a **bright**, sunny day. • What a great **April Fool**'s Day! • In English class, we **shouted** "Look, a mouse!" • The English teacher **ran** out the door. • But we **lied**. • It was just a **hamster**, not a **mouse**. • One of the kids in class **brought** it to school.

During the **break**, we **poured** oil on the floor. • We **rubbed** the floor hard. • We tried to make it **slippery**. • Finally, the history teacher **entered** the classroom. • I became **anxious**. • I **hardly** smiled.

What if he loses his **balance** and slips? • Should I call an **ambulance**? • He neither **slipped** nor became angry. • He smiled and **stopped** our tricks. • Was he able to think **ahead** and expect our **trick**?

다이어리에게,
환하고 햇살이 좋은 날이었어. 정말 멋진 만우절이었어! 영어 수업시간에 우리는□보세요, 쥐에요!□ 라고 외쳤어. 영어 선생님은 문 밖으로 뛰어나갔어. 하지만 우리는 거짓말했어. 그것은 쥐가 아니라 햄스터였어. 반 아이 중 한 명이 학교로 그것을 가져왔어.
쉬는 시간에 우리는 바닥에 기름을 부었어. 우리는 바닥을 열심히 문질렀어. 우리는 바닥을 미끄럽게 하려고 했어. 드디어 역사 선생님이 교실로 들어오셨어. 나는 걱정이 되었어. 나는 거의 웃지 않았어. 만약 선생님이 균형을 잃고 넘어지시면 어떻게 하지? 구급차를 불러야 할까? 그분은 넘어지지도 화를 내지도 않으셨어. 선생님은 미소를 지으셨고 우리의 장난을 중단시켰어. 그분은 앞을 생각하고 우리의 장난을 예상할 수 있었을까?

## bright
[bráit]
a. 밝은, 환한

It was a bright, sunny day.
환하고 햇살이 좋은 날이었어.

## April Fool
[éiprəl fú:l]
4월의 바보

What a great April Fool's Day!
정말 멋진 만우절이었어!
- April Fool's Day 만우절(4월 1일)

## shout
[ʃáut]
v. 외치다

In English class, we shouted "Look, a mouse!"
영어 수업시간에 우리는 "보세요, 쥐에요!"라고 외쳤어.
- shout - shouted - shouted

## run
[rʌ́n]
v. 달리다, 뛰다

The English teacher ran out the door.
영어 선생님은 문 밖으로 뛰어나갔어.
- run out 뛰어나가다
- run - ran - run

## lie
[lái]
v. 거짓말하다 n. 거짓말

But we lied.
하지만 우리는 거짓말했어.
- liar n. 거짓말쟁이  • tell a lie 거짓말하다
- lie - lied - lied

## hamster
[hǽmstər]
n. 햄스터

It was just a hamster, not a mouse.
그것은 쥐가 아니라 햄스터였어.

## mouse
[máus]
n. 생쥐

It was just a hamster, not a mouse.
그것은 쥐가 아니라 햄스터였어.

## bring
[bríŋ]
v. 가져오다

One of the kids in class brought it to school.

반 아이 중 한 명이 학교로 그것을 가져왔어.

- bring - brought - brought

## break
[bréik]
n. 쉬는 시간

During the break, we poured oil on the floor.

쉬는 시간에 우리는 바닥에 기름을 부었어.

## pour
[pɔ́ːr]
v. 붓다

During the break, we poured oil on the floor.

쉬는 시간에 우리는 바닥에 기름을 부었어.

- pour - poured - poured

## rub
[rʌ́b]
v. 문지르다

We rubbed the floor hard.

우리는 바닥을 열심히 문질렀어.

- rub - rubbed - rubbed

## slippery
[slípəri]
a. 미끄러운

We tried to make it slippery.

우리는 그것을 미끄럽게 하려고 했어.

- slip   v. 미끄러지다

## enter
[éntər]
v. 들어오다

Finally, the history teacher entered the classroom.

드디어 역사 선생님이 교실로 들어오셨어.

- entrance   n. 입장, 입구
- enter - entered - entered

## anxious
[ǽŋkʃəs]
a. 근심하는

I became anxious.

나는 걱정이 되었어.

- anxiety   n. 근심

Chapter 7. People

## hardly
[háːrdli]
ad. 거의 ~하지 않다

I hardly smiled.
나는 거의 웃지 않았어.
- hard  ad. 열심히, 세게

## balance
[bǽləns]
n. 균형  v. 균형을 잡다

What if he loses his balance and slips?
만약 선생님이 균형을 잃고 넘어지시면 어떻게 하지?
- lose one's balance  균형을 잃다
- keep one's balance  균형을 유지하다

## ambulance
[ǽmbjuləns]
n. 구급차

Should I call an ambulance?
내가 구급차를 불러야 할까?

## slip
[slíp]
v. 미끄러지다

He neither slipped nor became angry.
그는 넘어지지도 화를 내지도 않으셨어.
- slip - slipped - slipped

## stop
[stáp]
v. 멈추게 하다  n. 중지

He smiled and stopped our tricks.
그는 미소를 지으셨고 우리의 장난을 중단시켰어.
- stop - stopped - stopped

## ahead
[əhéd]
ad. 앞으로, 앞에

Was he able to think ahead and expect our trick?
그는 앞을 생각하고 우리의 장난을 예상할 수 있었을까?

## trick
[trík]
n. 장난, 속임수, 재주

Was he able to think ahead and expect our trick?
그는 앞을 생각하고 우리의 장난을 예상할 수 있었을까?

# Check Again!

**A** Translate each word or expression into Korean.

1. shout .....................
2. lie .....................
3. trick .....................
4. bring .....................
5. pour .....................
6. rub .....................
7. slippery .....................
8. enter .....................
9. anxious .....................
10. balance .....................

**B** Translate each word or expression into English.

1. 4월의 바보 .....................
2. 뛰어나가다 .....................
3. 쉬는 시간 .....................
4. 구급차 .....................
5. 거의 ~하지 않다 .....................

**C** Fill in the blank with the appropriate word. Refer to the Korean.

1. I r_____ the lotion on my skin.
   나는 그 로션을 피부에 문지렀어요.

2. The comedian s_____ on the floor.
   그 코미디언은 바닥에 미끄러졌어요.

3. I was too afraid to try to s_____ the fight.
   나는 싸움을 말리려고 하기에 너무 겁이 났어요.

4. I'll run a_____ and clear any objects in the way.
   내가 앞으로 뛰어가서 길에 놓인 물건들을 치울게요.

5. Tony b_____ his pet iguana in a cage to show his friends.
   토니는 친구들에게 보여주기 위해서 애완용 이구아나를 우리 안에 넣어 데리고 왔어요.

# Chapter 7
# People

Unit 16. Dad, don't forget your New Year's resolutions.

go on a holiday

exercise before bed

quit smoking

teach **how to use** chopsticks

# Episode

Bomi: I'm glad mom went on a **holiday** with her friends.

Dad: Yes, she will be **single** again for two days!

Bomi: Dad, read this **copy**. • It's your New Year's **resolutions**. • Mom wants you to **sign** it.

Dad: "I will **exercise** before bed." • "I will stop **smoking**." • Ugh, your mom is **like** my **manager**!

Bomi: Exercise and you can eat **double** cheeseburgers sometimes. • **Quit** smoking and you can have **slices** of sweet pies, too. • By your next **checkup**, you'll feel much better!

Dad: Your resolution is to help with the **chores**, right?

Bomi: Yes. Seri, Hoony and I will **divide** the work. • I'll take out the **garbage**. • Seri will water the **plants**. • And Hoony will clean the **garage**. • I'm also teaching Hoony how to use **chopsticks** right now.

Dad: Your mom will be very **pleased**.

---

보미: 저는 엄마가 친구들과 휴가를 떠나서 기뻐요.
아빠: 그래, 엄마는 이틀 동안 다시 혼자가 되는 거다!
보미: 아빠, 이 복사본을 읽어 보세요. 아빠의 새해 각오들이에요. 엄마는 아빠가 거기에 서명하기를 바라요.
아빠: □나는 잠자리에 들기 전에 운동을 할 것이다.□나는 담배를 끊을 것이다.□으, 네 엄마는 내 매니저 같구나!
보미: 운동을 하면 가끔 더블 치즈버거를 먹을 수 있어요. 담배를 끊으면 달콤한 파이도 먹을 수 있어요. 아빠의 다음 검진 때까지 몸이 훨씬 좋아질 거예요!
아빠: 너의 새해 각오는 가사를 돕는 거지, 그렇지?
보미: 네, 세리, 후니와 제가 일을 나눌 거예요. 저는 쓰레기를 내놓을 거예요. 세리는 식물에 물을 줄 거예요. 그리고 후니는 차고를 청소할 거예요. 지금 저는 후니에게 젓가락 사용법을 알려주고도 있어요.
아빠: 엄마가 무척 좋아하겠구나.

## holiday
[hálədèi]
n. 휴일, 휴가

I'm glad mom went on a holiday with her friends.
저는 엄마가 친구들과 휴가를 떠나서 기뻐요.
- go on a holiday  휴가를 가다

## single
[síŋgəl]
a. 혼자의, 독신의

Yes, she will be single again for two days!
그래, 그녀는 이틀 동안 다시 혼자가 되는 거다!

## copy
[kápi]
n. 사본, 복사한 것

Dad, read this copy.
아빠, 이 복사본을 읽어 보세요.

## resolution
[rèzəlúːʃən]
n. 결심, 결의

It's your New Year's resolutions.
아빠의 새해 각오들이에요.
- resolute  a. 굳게 결심한, 단호한
- New Year's resolution  새해 각오(결심)

## sign
[sáin]
v. 서명하다

Mom wants you to sign it.
엄마는 아빠가 거기에 서명하기를 바라요.
- signature  n. 서명, 사인
- sign - signed - signed

## exercise
[éksərsàiz]
v. 운동하다  n. 운동

I will exercise before bed.
나는 잠자리에 들기 전에 운동을 할 것이다.
- exercise - exercised - exercised

## smoke
[smóuk]
v. 담배를 피우다

I will stop smoking.
나는 담배를 끊을 것이다.
- smoke - smoked - smoked

## like
[làik]
prep. ~와 같이, ~처럼

Ugh, your mom is like my manager!
으, 네 엄마는 내 매니저 같구나!

## manager
[mǽnidʒər]
n. 매니저, 관리자

Ugh, your mom is like my manager!
으, 네 엄마는 내 매니저 같구나!

## double
[dʌ́bəl]
a. 두 배의, 2중의

Exercise and you can eat double cheeseburgers sometimes.
운동을 하면 가끔 더블 치즈버거를 먹을 수 있어요.

## quit
[kwít]
v. 그만두다, 끊다

Quit smoking and you can have slices of sweet pies, too.
담배를 끊으면 달콤한 파이도 먹을 수 있어요.
- quit - quit - quit

## slice
[sláis]
n. 얇게 썬 조각

Quit smoking and you can have slices of sweet pies, too.
담배를 끊으면 달콤한 파이도 먹을 수 있어요.

## checkup
[tʃékʌ̀p]
n. 건강 진단

By your next checkup, you'll feel much better!
다음 검진 때까지 몸이 훨씬 좋아질 거예요!

## chores
[tʃɔ́ːrz]
n. 가사, 자질구레한 일

Your resolution is to help with the chores, right?
너의 새해 각오는 가사를 돕는 거지, 그렇지?

## divide
[diváid]
v. 나누다

Yes. Seri, Hoony and I will divide the work.
네, 세리, 후니와 제가 일을 나눌 거예요.
- division   n. 분배, 분할
- divide - divided - divided

## garbage
[gáːrbidʒ]
n. 쓰레기

I'll take out the garbage.
저는 쓰레기를 내놓을 거예요.

## plant
[plǽnt]
n. 식물

Seri will water the plants.
세리는 식물에 물을 줄 거예요.

## garage
[gəráːʒ]
n. 차고

And Hoony will clean the garage.
그리고 후니는 차고를 청소할 거예요.

## chopsticks
[tʃɑ́pstìks]
n. 젓가락

I'm also teaching Hoony how to use chopsticks right now.
지금 저는 후니에게 젓가락 사용법을 알려주고도 있어요.

## pleased
[plíːzd]
a. 좋아하는, 기쁜

Your mom will be very pleased.
엄마가 무척 좋아하겠구나.
- please   v. 기쁘게 하다
- pleasure   n. 즐거움, 기쁨

# Check Again!

**A** Translate each word or expression into Korean.

1. holiday ..................
2. garage ..................
3. resolution ..................
4. sign ..................
5. plant ..................
6. smoke ..................
7. quit ..................
8. manager ..................
9. chores ..................
10. garbage ..................

**B** Translate each word or expression into English.

1. 사본, 복사한 것 ..................
2. 두 배의, 2중의 ..................
3. 건강 진단 ..................
4. 나누다 ..................
5. ~와 같이, ~처럼 ..................

**C** Fill in the blank with the appropriate word. Refer to the Korean.

1. Would you like another s_____ of this cheesecake?
   치즈케이크를 한 조각 더 드릴까요?

2. Aunt Betty is almost forty and still s_____.
   베티 이모는 거의 마흔 살인데 아직도 독신이에요.

3. Dad always says he will e_____ more, but he never does.
   아빠는 운동을 더 하겠다고 항상 말씀하시지만 결코 그렇지 않아요.

4. On Sundays, everyone helps out with the house c_____.
   일요일에는 모두 집안일을 도와요.

5. I'm so p_____ that you could make it to my party.
   네가 내 파티에 올 수 있어서 정말 기분이 좋아.

# Chapter 7
# People

Unit 17. I envy Sujin's aunt.

have a photo taken

interview someone

wrap a T-shirt

look **from a distance**

# Episode

**Bomi:** Sujin, is this a photo of the Volcanoes, my **favorite** music band? • Wow, they are very **stylish**. • And Youngwoong is really **awesome**.

**Sujin:** I had my **photo** taken with them. • My aunt works for a **broadcasting** company. • She is a **reporter**.

**Bomi:** Does she sometimes **interview** them?

**Sujin:** Of course.

**Bomi:** I really **envy** her. • Can she **deliver** a present for me?

**Sujin:** Well...

**Bomi:** I **wrapped** a T-shirt for Youngwoong. • And this is a **congratulation** card for his birthday.

**Sujin:** Why don't you give it to him in **person**?

**Bomi:** You know I'm not **brave**. • I don't have the **courage** to give it to Youngwoong. • **Honestly**, I couldn't say anything when I met them before. • I just looked at them from a **distance**. • I don't want to look **foolish** again.

Sujin **boasted** a bit in front of me. • Actually, she knows **exactly** how much I like the Volcanoes. • I hope she can **help** me.

보미: 수진, 이거 내가 좋아하는 음악 밴드 볼케이노 사진이니? 우와, 정말 맵시 있다. 그리고 영웅은 정말 멋져.
수진: 나는 그들과 함께 사진을 찍었어. 우리 고모가 방송국에서 일하시거든. 기자야.
보미: 가끔 그들을 인터뷰도 해?
수진: 물론이지.
보미: 정말 부럽다. 나 대신 선물을 전해 줄 수 있을까?
수진: 글쎄…
보미: 내가 영웅을 위해 티셔츠를 포장했어. 그리고 이것은 그의 생일 축하 카드야.
수진: 그에게 직접 주지 그래?
보미: 너도 알다시피 나는 용감하지 못해. 나는 영웅에게 그것을 줄 용기가 없어. 솔직히 나는 전에 그들을 만났을 때 한 마디도 못했어. 단지 먼 거리에서 바라만 보았어. 또다시 바보처럼 보이고 싶지 않아.

수진은 내 앞에서 약간 자랑했다. 사실 그 애는 내가 얼마나 볼케이노를 좋아하는지 정확하게 안다. 나는 그 애가 나를 도울 수 있기를 바란다.

## favorite
[féivərit]
a. 좋아하는

Sujin, is this a photo of the Volcanoes, my favorite music band?
수진, 이거 내가 좋아하는 음악 밴드 볼케이노 사진이니?

## stylish
[stáiliʃ]
a. 맵시 있는, 멋진

Wow, they are very stylish.
우와, 정말 맵시 있다.
- style  n. 스타일

## awesome
[ɔ́:səm]
a. 멋진, 굉장한

And Youngwoong is really awesome.
그리고 영웅은 정말 멋져.
- awe  n. 경외, 경외심

## photo
[fóutou]
n. 사진

I had my photo taken with them.
나는 그들과 함께 사진을 찍었어.
- photographer  n. 사진사

## broadcasting
[brɔ́:dkæstiŋ]
n. 방송

My aunt works for a broadcasting company.
우리 고모가 방송국에서 일하시거든.

## reporter
[ripɔ́:rtər]
n. 기자

She is a reporter.
그녀는 기자야.
- report  v. 보도하다  n. 보도, 보고(서)

## interview
[íntərvjù:]
v. 인터뷰하다

Does she sometimes interview them?
그녀는 가끔 그들을 인터뷰 해?
- interview - interviewed - interviewed

## envy
[énvi]
v. 부러워하다, 질투하다
n. 질투, 선망

I really envy her.
그녀가 정말 부럽다.
- envious  a. 질투가 많은
- envy - envied - envied

## deliver
[dilívər]
v. 전하다, 배달하다

Can she deliver a present for me?
나 대신 선물을 전해 줄 수 있을까?
- delivery  n. 배달
- deliver - delivered - delivered

## wrap
[ræp]
v. 포장하다

I wrapped a T-shirt for Youngwoong.
내가 영웅을 위해 티셔츠를 포장했어.
- wrap - wrapped - wrapped

## congratulation
[kəngrætʃəléiʃən]
n. 축하

And this is a congratulation card for his birthday.
그리고 이것은 그의 생일 축하 카드야.
- congratulate  v. 축하하다

## person
[pə́:rsən]
n. 사람, 개인

Why don't you give it to him in person?
네가 그에게 직접 주지 그래?
- personal  a. 개인적인   · in person  직접

## brave
[bréiv]
a. 용감한

You know I'm not brave.
너도 알다시피 나는 용감하지 못해.
- bravery  n. 용기   · bravely  ad. 용감하게

## courage
[kə́:ridʒ]
n. 용기

I don't have the courage to give it to Youngwoong.
나는 영웅에게 그것을 줄 용기가 없어.
- encourage  v. 격려하다
- courageous  a. 용감한

## honestly
[ánistli]
ad. 솔직히

Honestly, I couldn't say anything when I met them before.
솔직히 나는 전에 그들을 만났을 때 한 마디도 못했어.
- honesty  n. 솔직함  • honest  a. 솔직한

## distance
[dístəns]
n. 먼 거리, 먼 곳, 거리

I just looked at them from a distance.
단지 먼 거리에서 바라만 보았어.
- distant  a. 거리가 떨어진, 먼

## foolish
[fú:liʃ]
a. 어리석은

I don't want to look foolish again.
또다시 바보처럼 보이고 싶지 않아.
- fool  n. 바보

## boast
[bóust]
v. 자랑하다

Sujin boasted a bit in front of me.
수진은 내 앞에서 약간 자랑했다.
- boastful  a. 자랑하는
- boast - boasted - boasted

## exactly
[igzǽktli]
ad. 정확하게

Actually, she knows exactly how much I like the Volcanoes.
사실 그녀는 내가 얼마나 볼케이노를 좋아하는지 정확하게 안다.
- exact  a. 정확한

## help
[hélp]
v. 돕다, 거들다
n. 도움

I hope she can help me.
나는 그녀가 나를 도울 수 있기를 바란다.
- help - helped - helped

# Check Again!

**A** Translate each word or expression into Korean.

1. boast .................
2. wrap .................
3. stylish .................
4. interview .................
5. envy .................
6. deliver .................
7. favorite .................
8. foolish .................
9. awesome .................
10. honestly .................

**B** Translate each word or expression into English.

1. 축하 .................
2. 먼 거리 .................
3. 방송 .................
4. 용감한 .................
5. 정확히 .................

**C** Fill in the blank with the appropriate word. Refer to the Korean.

1. The boy doesn't have enough c_____ to ride the roller coaster.
   그 남자아이는 롤러코스터를 탈만큼 충분히 용기가 없다.

2. I gave it to her in p_____.
   나는 그녀에게 직접 그것을 주었다.

3. Yesterday's weather r_____ was wrong.
   어제의 날씨를 보도한 기자는 틀렸다.

4. The d_____ from my house to school is far.
   나의 집에서 학교까지의 거리는 멀다.

5. The other team showed e_____ because we won the game.
   상대팀은 우리가 게임을 이겨서 질투했다.

Chapter 7. People  **135**

# Chapter 7
# People

Unit 18. I remember the first day we met.

move to the same **elementary** school

sit **next to** someone

look alike

**be good at** spreading jam evenly

# Episode

Dear Sara,

Do you **remember** when we first met? • We moved to the same **elementary** school. • We even came to school on the same **date**. • **Naturally** we became friends. • **Suppose** we were not in the same classroom, who would have been my friend? • You sat next to me. • We don't look **alike** at all, but our **classmates** said we did. • We are **different** in some ways. • You have good **sense** for cooking, but I don't. • I like your toast and you can make it without **burning** it. • You are also good at **spreading** jam **evenly**. • You're a bit shy, but I'm **outgoing**. You are very **friendly** to me. • We are **similar** in some ways, too. • We like the same **programs**. • **During** our **spare** time, we enjoy acting. • **Sometimes** we pretend we are in a **spaceship**. • Sara, never **forget** your promise to go to the South Pole with me in the **future**.

---

사라에게,

우리가 처음 만났을 때 기억하니? 우리는 같은 초등학교로 전학을 왔어. 심지어 같은 날짜에 학교에 왔어. 자연스럽게 우리는 친구가 되었어. 만일 우리가 같은 학급이 아니었으면 누가 내 친구가 되었을까? 너는 내 옆에 앉았어. 우리는 생김새가 닮지 않았는데 우리 반 애들은 우리가 그렇다고 말했어. 우리는 어떤 면에서는 달라. 너는 요리에 감각이 있지만, 나는 없어. 나는 너의 **토스트를 좋아하**고 너는 그것을 태우지 않고 만들 수 있어. 너는 또한 잼을 고르게 바르는 것을 잘해. 너는 약간 부끄러움을 타지만, 나는 외향적이야. 너는 내게 아주 친절해. 우리는 어떤 점에서는 비슷해. 우리는 같은 프로그램들을 좋아해. 우리는 여가 시간에 연기하는 것을 즐겨. 가끔 우리는 우주선을 탄 척을 하지. 사라, 미래에 나와 함께 남극에 가자고 한 약속을 절대 잊지 마.

### remember
[rimémbər]
v. 기억하다

Do you remember when we first met?
우리가 처음 만났을 때 기억하니?
- remembrance  n. 기억, 추억
- remember - remembered - remembered

### elementary
[èləméntəri]
a. 초등학교의, 입문의

We moved to the same elementary school.
우리는 같은 초등학교로 전학을 왔어.

### date
[déit]
n. 날짜

We even came to school on the same date.
심지어 같은 날짜에 학교에 왔어.
- dated  a. 날짜가 있는

### naturally
[nætʃərəli]
ad. 자연스럽게, 당연히

Naturally we became friends.
자연스럽게 우리는 친구가 되었어.
- nature  n. 자연  • natural  a. 자연스러운

### suppose
[səpóuz]
v. 가정하다, 만약 ~이면, 어떨까

Suppose we were not in the same classroom, who would have been my friend?
만일 우리가 같은 학급이 아니었으면 누가 내 친구가 되었을까?
- suppose - supposed - supposed

### alike
[əláik]
a. 비슷한, 서로 같은

We don't look alike at all, but our classmates said we did.
우리는 생김새가 닮지 않았는데 우리 반 애들은 우리가 그렇다고 말했어.

### classmate
[klǽsmèit]
n. 반친구, 급우

We don't look alike at all, but our classmates said we did.
우리는 생김새가 닮지 않았는데 우리 반 애들은 우리가 그렇다고 말했어.

## different
[dífərənt]
a. 다른

We are different in some ways.
우리는 어떤 면에서는 달라.
- difference  n. 차이(점)
- differently  ad. 다르게

## sense
[séns]
n. 감각

You have good sense for cooking, but I don't.
너는 요리에 감각이 있지만, 나는 없어.
- sensory  a. 감각의  • sensitive  a. 민감한
- sensible  a. 분별 있는, 느낄 수 있는

## burn
[bə́ːrn]
v. 태우다

I like your toast and you can make it without burning it.
나는 너의 토스트를 좋아하고 너는 그것을 태우지 않고 만들 수 있어.
- burn - burned/burnt - burned/ burnt

## spread
[spréd]
v. 바르다, 펴다

You are also good at spreading jam evenly.
너는 또한 잼을 고르게 바르는 것을 잘해.
- spread - spread - spread

## evenly
[íːvənli]
ad. 고르게, 평평하게

You are also good at spreading jam evenly.
너는 또한 잼을 고르게 바르는 것을 잘해.
- even  a. 평평한, 고른

## outgoing
[áutgòuiŋ]
a. 외향적인

You're a bit shy, but I'm outgoing.
너는 약간 부끄러움을 타지만, 나는 외향적이야.

## friendly
[fréndli]
a. 친절한

You are very friendly to me.
너는 내게 아주 친절해.
- friend  n. 친구

Chapter 7. People  **139**

## similar
[símələr]
a. 유사한

We are similar in some ways, too.
우리는 어떤 점에서는 비슷해.
- similarity　n. 유사함　• similarly　ad. 유사하게

## program
[próugræm]
n. 프로그램

We like the same programs.
우리는 같은 프로그램들을 좋아해.

## during
[djúəriŋ]
prep. ~동안

During our spare time, we enjoy acting.
우리는 여가 시간에 연기하는 것을 즐겨.

## spare
[spɛər]
a. 여분의

During our spare time, we enjoy acting.
우리는 여가 시간에 연기하는 것을 즐겨.

## sometimes
[sʌ́mtàimz]
ad. 가끔

Sometimes we pretend we are in a spaceship.
가끔 우리는 우주선을 탄 척 하지.

## spaceship
[spéisʃìp]
n. 우주선

Sometimes we pretend we are in a spaceship.
가끔 우리는 우주선을 탄 척 하지.

## forget
[fərgét]
v. 잊다

Sara, never forget your promise to go to the South Pole with me in the future.
사라, 미래에 나와 함께 남극에 가자고 한 약속을 절대 잊지 마.
- forgetful　a. 잘 잊어버리는　• forgettable　a. 잊기 쉬운
- forget - forgot - forgot/forgotten

## future
[fjúːtʃər]
n. 미래, 앞날

Sara, never forget your promise to go to the South Pole with me in the future.
사라, 미래에 나와 함께 남극에 가자고 한 약속을 절대 잊지 마.

# Check Again!

**A** Translate each word or expression into Korean.

1. suppose ........................
2. evenly ........................
3. sense ........................
4. forget ........................
5. remember ........................
6. naturally ........................
7. spread ........................
8. burn ........................
9. alike ........................
10. different ........................

**B** Translate each word or expression into English.

1. 날짜 ........................
2. 유사한 ........................
3. 가끔 ........................
4. 미래 ........................
5. ~동안 ........................

**C** Fill in the blank with the appropriate word. Refer to the Korean.

1. I have various types of friends because I am an o_____ person.
   나는 외향적인 사람이기 때문에 다양한 종류의 친구들이 있다.

2. The new student was sent to the e_____ level class.
   새로운 학생은 입문 수준의 반으로 보내졌다.

3. A nice neighbor lent a s_____ tire for us to use.
   친절한 이웃이 우리가 사용할 수 있도록 여분의 타이어를 빌려주었다.

4. The shape of her face and an egg are a_____.
   그녀의 얼굴 형태와 달걀의 형태는 서로 같다.

5. Our class president was elected because of his f_____ personality.
   우리 반 반장은 친절한 성격 덕분에 선출되었다.

## Chapter 7. People

# Appearance

1. **curly hair** 곱슬머리
2. **straight hair** 직모
3. **T-shirt** 티셔츠
4. **skirt** 치마
5. **suit** 정장
6. **high heels** 하이힐
7. **sneakers** 운동화
8. **handbag** 핸드백
9. **shoulder bag** 어깨에 매는 가방
10. **blouse** 블라우스
11. **dress shirt** 정장용 셔츠
12. **tie** 타이

Amanda has **blond hair**.
아만다는 금발 머리를 하고 있습니다.

She is wearing a **skirt** and a **T-shirt**.
그녀는 치마와 티셔츠를 입고 있어요.

Amy is **slim** and **tall**.
에이미는 날씬하고 키가 커요.

She is wearing a **suit** and **high heels**.
그녀는 정장과 하이힐을 신고 있어요.

David is **big** and has big **muscles**.
데이비드는 덩치가 크고 근육이 많아요.

He is wearing **sneakers**.
그는 운동화를 신고 있어요.

Mr. Brown is **fat** and has **curly hair**.
브라운 씨는 뚱뚱하고 곱슬머리예요.

He is wearing a **dress shirt** and a **tie**.
그는 정장용 셔츠를 입고 타이를 매고 있어요.

## Culture Plus

### Personalities 성격

| | |
|---|---|
| +dynamic 동적인 | +selfish 이기적인 |
| +bold 대담한 | +shy 수줍음을 타는, 내성적인 |
| +cheerful 쾌활한 | +talkative 수다스런 |
| +diligent 부지런한 | +timid 소심한, 겁 많은 |
| +friendly 친절한, 다정한 | +witty 재치가 있는 |
| +gentle 신사다운 | |
| +outgoing 외향적인 | |

Chapter 7. People

# STORYTELLING VOCABULARY
## GREEN

## Chapter 8. History, Art, and Culture

**Unit 19.** Seri designed her own bandage.

**Unit 20.** Hoony has a bubble show.

**Unit 21.** Grandpa explained some historical changes.

# Chapter 8
# History, Art, and Culture

Unit 19. Seri designed her own bandage.

**cut one's finger**

**draw a** neat **pattern**

**add** some beads

**send a picture**

# Episode

S e r i: Ouch, I **cut** my finger. • Look, there is **blood**!

Bomi: I'll get the **first-aid** kit. • Here, put this **bandage** on it.

S e r i: That one is so **plain** and **simple**. • I'm going to **draw** something on it.

Bomi: Why don't you draw some **hot dogs**?

S e r i: That's **gross**. • No, I'll draw a really neat **pattern**. • Isn't it **beautiful**? • And I want to **add** some beads.

Bomi: I'll help you **glue** them on.

S e r i: Thanks. Hey, get the **digital camera** for me.

Bomi: Are you going to **post** a picture on YouTube?

S e r i: No, I want to **send** it to a bandage **company**. • It might **impress** them.

Bomi: I **guess** it could help their **business**.

---

세리: 아야, 손가락을 베었어! 이봐, 피가 나!
보미: 내가 구급상자를 가져올게. 자 여기, 거기에 이 반창고를 붙여.
세리: 그것은 너무 평범하고 단순해. 나는 그 위에 무언가를 그릴래.
보미: 핫도그를 좀 그리는 게 어때?
세리: 그건 정말 싫어. 아니, 나는 아주 멋진 무늬를 그릴 거야. 이거 아름답지 않아? 그리고 나는 구슬을 좀 추가하고 싶어.
보미: 네가 그걸 붙일 수 있게 도와줄게.
세리: 고마워. 내게 디카를 가져다 줘.
보미: 유튜브에 사진을 올릴 거니?
세리: 아니, 나는 그것을 반창고 회사에 보내고 싶어. 그들에게 깊은 인상을 줄지도 모르잖아.
보미: 그것이 그들의 사업에 도움이 될 수 있을 거라고 생각해.

## cut
[kʌt]
v. 베다, 상처를 내다  n. 베기

Ouch, I cut my finger.
아야, 손가락을 베었어!
- cut - cut - cut

## blood
[blʌd]
n. 피

Look, there is blood!
이봐, 피가 나!
- bleed  v. 피가 나다

## first-aid
[fə́ːrstéid]
a. 응급 치료의

I'll get the first-aid kit.
내가 구급상자를 가져올게.

## bandage
[bǽndidʒ]
n. 반창고

Here, put this bandage on it.
자 여기, 거기에 이 반창고를 붙여.

## plain
[pléin]
a. 평범한, 단조로운

That one is so plain and simple.
그것은 너무 평범하고 단순해.

## simple
[símpl]
a. 단순한, 간단한

That one is so plain and simple.
그것은 너무 평범하고 단순해.
- simplify  v. 간단하게 하다

## draw
[drɔː]
v. 그리다

I'm going to draw something on it.
나는 그 위에 무언가를 그릴래.
- draw - drew - drawn

## hot dog
[hát dɔ̀(:)g]
n. 핫도그

Why don't you draw some hot dogs?
핫도그를 좀 그리는 게 어때?

## gross
[gróus]
a. 불쾌한, 구역질 나는

That's gross.
그건 정말 싫어.

## pattern
[pǽtərn]
n. 무늬

No, I'll draw a really neat pattern.
아니, 나는 아주 멋진 무늬를 그릴 거야.

## beautiful
[bjúːtəfəl]
a. 아름다운

Isn't it beautiful?
이거 아름답지 않아?

- beauty  n. 아름다움

## add
[ǽd]
v. 추가하다, 더하다

And I want to add some beads.
그리고 나는 구슬을 좀 추가하고 싶어.

- add - added - added

## glue
[glúː]
v. 접착제로 붙이다  n. 접착제

I'll help you glue them on.
네가 그걸 붙일 수 있게 도와줄게.

- glue - glued - glued

## digital camera
[dídʒitl kǽmərə]
디카(디지털 카메라)

Thanks. Hey, get the digital camera for me.
고마워. 내게 디카를 가져다 줘.

## post
[póust]
v. 게시하다, 정보를 알리다

Are you going to post a picture on YouTube?
유튜브에 사진을 올릴 거니?

- post - posted - posted

## send
[sénd]
v. 보내다

No, I want to send it to a bandage company.
아니, 나는 그것을 반창고 회사에 보내고 싶어.

- send - sent - sent

## company
[kʌ́mpəni]
n. 회사

No, I want to send it to a bandage company.
아니, 나는 그것을 반창고 회사에 보내고 싶어.

## impress
[imprés]
v. 깊은 인상을 주다

It might impress them.
그들에게 깊은 인상을 줄지도 모르잖아.

- impression  n. 인상  · impressive  a. 인상적인
- impress - impressed - impressed

## guess
[gés]
v. 추측하다, 알아맞히다

I guess it could help their business.
나는 그것이 그들의 사업에 도움이 될 수 있을 거라고 생각해.

- guess - guessed - guessed

## business
[bíznis]
n. 사업

I guess it could help their business.
나는 그것이 그들의 사업에 도움이 될 수 있을 거라고 생각해.

# Check Again!

**A** Translate each word or expression into Korean.

1. cut ........................
2. blood ........................
3. first-aid ........................
4. simple ........................
5. gross ........................
6. beautiful ........................
7. post ........................
8. company ........................
9. impress ........................
10. pattern ........................

**B** Translate each word or expression into English.

1. 반창고 ........................
2. 그리다 ........................
3. 보내다 ........................
4. 추가하다 ........................
5. 접착제로 붙이다 ........................

**C** Fill in the blank with the appropriate word. Refer to the Korean.

1. We took nearly a hundred shots on our d_____ camera.
   우리는 디지털 카메라로 거의 백 장 정도 찍었어요.

2. I can't g_____ other people's age very well.
   나는 다른 사람의 나이를 잘 못 맞춰요.

3. My uncle has been in the fashion b_____ for 10 years.
   우리 삼촌은 10년 동안 패션업계에서 일해 왔어요.

4. We were i_____ by the performance of the amateur B-boys.
   우리는 그 아마추어 비보이들의 공연에 깊은 감동을 받았어요.

5. The quiet boy liked to wear p_____ clothes.
   그 조용한 남자아이는 평범한 옷을 입기를 좋아했다.

# Chapter 8
# History, Art, and Culture

## Unit 20. Hoony has a bubble show.

**blow bubbles**

**make finger shadows**

**create a hyena**

**use one's brain**

# Episode

Dear Diary,

I see Hoony **blowing** soap **bubbles**. • I'll **count** them. • He blew ten **round** bubbles. • He also blew some **flat** bubbles. • He can make other **shapes**, too. • He is **practicing** for his bubble show. • Sara and I are going to make finger **shadows** for him. • We will also be his **voice actors**. • We are going to be behind a **screen**.

Bomi: The show is going to be on **schedule**, right? • Watch us **create** a hyena.

Hoony: Are those its **sharp** teeth?

Bomi: Yes, it's eating **rotten** meat. • The meat **bone** was hard to make.

Hoony: Yeah, you really used your **brains**!

Bomi: Now, look at us make tree **branches**.

Hoony: Neat! Oh, look at all the **students** at the **gate**.

Bomi: Don't worry. They'll think you're a **professional**!

---

다이어리에게,
후니가 비눗방울을 부는 모습이 보여. 내가 그것들을 세어볼게. 그는 둥근 비눗방울을 열 개 불었어. 납작한 비눗방울도 몇 개 불었어. 그는 다른 모양도 만들 수 있어. 그는 자신의 비눗방울 쇼를 위해 연습하고 있어. 사라와 나는 그를 위해 손가락 그림자를 만들어 줄 거야. 우리는 그의 성우도 되어 줄 거야. 우리는 막 뒤에 있을 거야.

보미: 쇼는 예정대로 진행될 거지, 그렇지? 우리가 하이에나를 만들어내는 것을 봐.
후니: 그것들이 하이에나의 날카로운 이빨이야?
보미: 응, 썩은 고기를 먹고 있어. 고기 뼈는 표현하기 힘들었어.
후니: 그래, 정말 머리를 썼네!
보미: 이제 우리가 나뭇가지를 표현하는 것을 봐.
후니: 멋지다! 아, 문 앞에 있는 저 많은 학생들을 봐.
보미: 걱정하지 마. 그들은 네가 전문가라고 생각할 거야!

## blow
[blóu]
v. 불다

I see Hoony blowing soap bubbles.
후니가 비눗방울을 부는 모습이 보여.
- blow - blew - blown

## bubble
[bʌ́bl]
n. 거품

I see Hoony blowing soap bubbles.
후니가 비눗방울을 부는 모습이 보여.

## count
[káunt]
v. 세다, 계산하다

I'll count them.
내가 그것들을 세어볼게.
- countable  a. 셀 수 있는
- count - counted - counted

## round
[ráund]
a. 둥근

He blew ten round bubbles.
그는 둥근 비눗방울을 열 개 불었어.

## flat
[flǽt]
a. 납작한

He also blew some flat bubbles.
그는 납작한 비눗방울도 몇 개 불었어.

## shape
[ʃéip]
n. 모양

He can make other shapes, too.
그는 다른 모양도 만들 수 있어.

## practice
[prǽktis]
v. 연습하다  n. 연습

He is practicing for his bubble show.
그는 자신의 비눗방울 쇼를 위해 연습하고 있어.
- practice - practiced - practiced

## shadow
[ʃǽdou]
n. 그림자

Sara and I are going to make finger shadows for him.
사라와 나는 그를 위해 손가락 그림자를 만들어 줄 거야.

## voice actor
[vɔ́is ǽktər]
성우

We will also be his voice actors.
우리는 그의 성우도 되어 줄 거야.

## screen
[skríːn]
n. 막, 휘장

We are going to be behind a screen.
우리는 막 뒤에 있을 거야.

## schedule
[skédʒu(ː)l]
n. 예정, 계획

The show is going to be on schedule, right?
쇼는 예정대로 진행될 거지, 그렇지?

- on schedule  예정대로
- ahead schedule  예정보다 먼저
- behind schedule  예정보다 늦게

## create
[kriːéit]
v. 만들어내다, 창작하다

Watch us create a hyena.
우리가 하이에나를 만들어내는 것을 봐.

- creation  n. 창작, 작품
- creative  a. 창조적인, 독창적인
- create - created - created

## sharp
[ʃɑːrp]
a. 날카로운

Are those its sharp teeth?
그것들이 그것의 날카로운 이빨이야?

Chapter 8. History, Art, and Culture

## rotten
[rátn]
a. 썩은

Yes, it's eating rotten meat.
응, 썩은 고기를 먹고 있어.

- rot  v. 썩다, 부패하다

## bone
[bóun]
n. 뼈

The meat bone was hard to make.
고기 뼈는 표현하기 힘들었어.

## brain
[bréin]
n. 뇌

Yeah, you really used your brains!
그래, 정말 머리를 썼네!

- use one's brain  머리를 쓰다, 지혜를 짜내다

## branch
[bræntʃ]
n. 가지

Now, look at us make tree branches.
이제 우리가 나뭇가지를 표현하는 것을 봐.

## student
[stjúːdənt]
n. 학생

Neat! Oh, look at all the students at the gate.
멋지다! 아, 문 앞에 있는 저 많은 학생들을 봐.

## gate
[géit]
n. 출입문

Neat! Oh, look at all the students at the gate.
멋지다! 아, 문 앞에 있는 저 많은 학생들을 봐.

## professional
[prəféʃənəl]
n. 전문가  a. 프로의

Don't worry. They'll think you're a professional!
걱정하지 마. 그들은 네가 전문가라고 생각할 거야!

# Check Again!

**A** Translate each word or expression into Korean.

1. blow _____
2. count _____
3. round _____
4. practice _____
5. shadow _____
6. voice actor _____
7. schedule _____
8. professional _____
9. rotten _____
10. bone _____

**B** Translate each word or expression into English.

1. 납작한 _____
2. 모양 _____
3. 막, 휘장 _____
4. 날카로운 _____
5. 가지 _____

**C** Fill in the blank with the appropriate word. Refer to the Korean.

1. We've been p_____ for this night for months.
   우리는 몇 개월 동안 이 밤을 위해 연습해 왔어요.

2. I wonder who c_____ the first donut.
   누가 최초의 도넛을 만들었는지 궁금해요.

3. The play will be on s_____.
   그 연극은 예정대로 진행될 거야.

4. Let's use our b_____ and find a solution.
   우리 머리를 써서 해결책을 찾아냅시다.

5. There are always two men guarding the g_____.
   항상 출입문을 지키는 남자가 두 명 있어요.

Chapter 8. History, Art, and Culture

# Chapter 8
# History, Art, and Culture

Unit 21. Grandpa explained some historical changes.

life **in the past**

**make** one's first **flight**

**invent** the telephone

change **conversations**

# Episode

Dear Diary,

Grandpa and I talked about life in the **past**. • I asked him about some changes that **occurred** in the last **century**. • He **explained** some of them to me.

Grandpa: We didn't go to the **dentist** to pull out teeth. • Can you **imagine** pulling them out at home?
Bomi: Oh, the **pain**! • Wasn't it **harmful** to people's health?
Grandpa: Not at all. • And we didn't get **regular** checkups, either. • There were many **historical** events in the 20th century. • The Wright brothers made their first **flight**.
Bomi: So they were the world's first **pilots**.
Grandpa: Yes. Cars began to be **mass-produced**. • Workers made them in **factories**. • Before, there were lots of **farmers**. • But soon, there were more factory **engineers**.
Bomi: And the telephone was a big change in **communication**, right?
Grandpa: Well, Alexander Graham Bell **invented** that a century **earlier**. • In the 20th century, cell phones changed **conversations**.

다이어리에게,
할아버지와 나는 과거의 생활에 대해 얘기를 나눴어. 나는 할아버지께 지난 세기에 있었던 몇 가지 변화에 대해 여쭤봤어. 그는 내게 몇 가지에 대해 설명해 주었어.
할아버지: 우리는 이를 뽑기 위해 치과 의사에게 가지 않았어. 집에서 이를 뽑았다는 게 상상이 되니?
보  미: 아, 고통스럽겠어요! 사람들 건강에 해롭지는 않았나요?
할아버지: 전혀 그렇지는 않았어. 그리고 우리는 정기적으로 검진을 받지도 않았어. 20세기에는 역사적인 사건이 많았어. 라이트 형제가 그들의 첫 비행을 했지.
보  미: 그럼 그들이 세계 최초의 조종사였군요.
할아버지: 맞아. 자동차가 대량생산되기 시작했어. 노동자들이 그것을 공장에서 만들었어. 전에는 농부가 많았어. 하지만 곧 공장 기술자가 더 많아졌지.
보  미: 그리고 전화기가 의사 소통에 있어서 큰 변화였어요, 그렇죠?
할아버지: 음, 알렉산더 그레이엄 벨은 한 세기 앞서 그것을 발명했어. 20세기에는 휴대 전화가 대화를 바꿔놓았어.

## past
[pǽst]
n. 과거

Grandpa and I talked about life in the past.
할아버지와 나는 과거의 생활에 대해 얘기를 나눴어.

## occur
[əkə́ːr]
v. 일어나다, 발생하다

I asked him about some changes that occurred in the last century.
나는 그에게 지난 세기에 있었던 변화에 대해 여쭤봤어.
- occurrence  n. 발생, 사건
- occur - occurred - occurred

## century
[séntʃuri]
n. 세기, 100년

I asked him about some changes that occurred in the last century.
나는 그에게 지난 세기에 있었던 변화에 대해 여쭤봤어.

## explain
[ikspléin]
v. 설명하다

He explained some of them to me.
그는 내게 몇 가지에 대해 설명해 주었어.
- explanation  n. 설명 • explanatory  a. 설명적인
- explain - explained - explained

## dentist
[déntist]
n. 치과 의사

We didn't go to the dentist to pull out teeth.
우리는 이를 뽑기 위해 치과 의사에게 가지 않았어.

## imagine
[imǽdʒin]
v. 상상하다

Can you imagine pulling them out at home?
집에서 그것을 뽑았다는 게 상상이 되니?
- imagination  n. 상상
- imaginary  a. 상상의, 가상의
- imaginative  a. 상상력이 풍부한
- imagine - imagined - imagined

## pain
[péin]
n. 고통

Oh, the pain!
아, 고통스럽겠어요!
- painful  a. 고통스러운

## harmful
[hɑ́ːrmfəl]
a. 해로운

Wasn't it harmful to people's health?
사람들 건강에 해롭지는 않았나요?

- harm  v. 해를 주다  n. 해로움

## regular
[régjələr]
a. 정기적인

And we didn't get regular checkups, either.
그리고 우리는 정기적으로 검진을 받지도 않았어.

## historical
[histɔ́(ː)rikəl]
a. 역사적인

There were many historical events in the 20th century.
20세기에는 역사적인 사건이 많았어.

- history  n. 역사

## flight
[fláit]
n. 비행

The Wright brothers made their first flight.
라이트 형제가 그들의 첫 비행을 했지.

- fly  v. 날다

## pilot
[páilət]
n. 조종사

So they were the world's first pilots.
그럼 그들이 세계 최초의 조종사였군요.

## mass-produce
[mǽsprədjúːs]
v. 대량 생산하다

Yes. Cars began to be mass-produced.
맞아. 자동차가 대량생산되기 시작했어.

- mass-produced  a. 대량 생산의
- mass-produce - mass-produced - mass-produced

Chapter 8. History, Art, and Culture

## factory
[fǽktəri]
n. 공장

Workers made them in factories.
노동자들이 그것을 공장에서 만들었어.

## farmer
[fáːrmər]
n. 농부

Before, there were lots of farmers.
전에는 농부가 많았어.

## engineer
[èndʒiníər]
n. 기술자

But soon, there were more factory engineers.
하지만 곧 공장 기술자가 더 많아졌지.

## communication
[kəmjùːnəkéiʃən]
n. 의사 소통

And the telephone was a big change in communication, right?
그리고 전화기가 의사 소통에 있어서 큰 변화였어요, 그렇죠?

- communicate   v. 의사 소통하다

## invent
[invént]
v. 발명하다

Well, Alexander Graham Bell invented that a century earlier.
음, 알렉산더 그레이엄 벨은 한 세기 앞서 그것을 발명했어.

- invention   n. 발명   • inventor   n. 발명가
- invent - invented - invented

## earlier
[ə́ːrliər]
ad. 일찍이, 예전에

Well, Alexander Graham Bell invented that a century earlier.
음, 알렉산더 그레이엄 벨은 한 세기 앞서 그것을 발명했어.

## conversation
[kànvərséiʃən]
n. 대화

In the 20th century, cell phones changed conversations.
20세기에는 휴대 전화가 대화를 바꿔놓았어.

- converse   v. 이야기하다

# Check Again!

**A** Translate each word or expression into Korean.

1. century ....................  2. explain ....................

3. occur ....................  4. invent ....................

5. regular ....................  6. historical ....................

7. flight ....................  8. mass-produce ....................

9. communication ....................  10. conversation ....................

**B** Translate each word or expression into English.

1. 과거 ....................

2. 치과 의사 ....................

3. 고통 ....................

4. 조종사 ....................

5. 일찍이, 예전에 ....................

**C** Fill in the blank with the appropriate word. Refer to the Korean.

1. This art museum used to be a paint f_____ .
   이 미술관은 예전에 페인트 공장이었어요.

2. He is the top e_____ at that computer company.
   그는 그 컴퓨터 회사의 최고 기술자에요.

3. I heard someone i_____ a laser gun to kill mosquitoes.
   나는 누군가가 모기를 죽이기 위한 레이저 총을 개발했다고 들었어요.

4. Can you i_____ jumping out of a flying plane?
   비행 중인 비행기에서 뛰어내리는 것을 상상할 수 있어요?

5. Don't worry. It's not h_____ to anyone.
   걱정 말아요. 그것은 어느 누구에게도 해롭지 않아요.

Chapter 8. History, Art, and Culture

# On Halloween

1. **pumpkin** 늙은 호박
2. **jack-o-lantern** 호박 초롱
3. **candle** 양초
4. **witch** 마녀
5. **broom** 빗자루
6. **trick or treat** 사탕 안주면 장난칠 거야
7. **mask** 가면
8. **candy** 사탕
9. **pirate** 해적
10. **costume party** 여러 가지 복장의 파티
11. **treats** 선물로 주는 사탕
12. **ghost** 유령

- There is a **costume party** on Halloween.
  할로윈에는 여러 가지 복장의 파티가 열린다.

- Jeremy is saying, "**Trick or treat**."
  제레미는 "사탕 안주면 장난칠 거야"라고 말하고 있다.

- Shiny is dressed up as a **ghost**.
  샤이니는 유령으로 분장을 했다.

- Jane is dressed up as a **princess**.
  제인은 공주 분장을 했다.

- Cindy is holding a **jack-o-lantern**.
  신디는 호박초롱을 들고 있다.

- Cindy is also holding a **broom**.
  신디는 또한 빗자루를 들고 있다.

- Sam is wearing a Batman **mask**.
  샘은 배트맨 가면을 쓰고 있다.

### Culture Plus

**Special Days** 특별한 날

- Christmas  크리스마스
- Parents' Day  어버이의 날
- April Fool's Day  만우절
- New Year's Day  새해 첫날
- Thanksgiving Day  추수 감사절
- Independence Day  독립기념일
- Columbus Day  콜럼버스의 날
- Arbor Day  식목일
- Memorial Day  현충일

# STORYTELLING VOCABULARY

## GREEN

## Chapter 9. Politics and Social Issues

**Unit 22.** My family volunteered at the ocean village.

**Unit 23.** Seri will design school uniforms for girls.

**Unit 24.** We add some lines to a song.

# Chapter 9
# Politics and Social Issues

Unit 22. My family volunteered at the ocean village.

**take a shower** with hot water

an **oil spill**

**rinse off** rocks

**show** one's **appreciation**

# Episode

D a d: Tomorrow we will leave for an ocean **village**. • It's **far** from Seoul.

Bomi: Dad, can we take a **shower** with hot water? • Can we have delicious **seafood** there?

D a d: Bomi, we're going to **volunteer** there.

Bomi: **Pardon**? • Volunteering on Christmas **Eve**? • Dad, are you talking like Jesus, "Love your **neighbors**?"

D a d: Bomi, there was an **oil spill**.

Dad **announced** the news suddenly at **dinner**. • We **reached** the village in the early morning. • Many people were **rinsing** off rocks. • Our family worked like a **team**. I found some birds on the **coast**. • Seri and I did **pair** work. • We cleaned oil from their **feathers**. • We worked hard and even skipped a **meal**. • At the end of the day, the villagers showed their **appreciation** to us. • Dad said, "Bomi and Seri, you were **really hardworking** today. I'm proud of you."

---

아빠: 내일 우리는 해안 마을로 떠날 거야. 그곳은 서울에서 멀리 떨어져 있어.
보미: 아빠, 뜨거운 물로 샤워할 수 있나요? 거기에서 맛있는 해산물을 먹을 수 있나요?
아빠: 보미, 우리는 자원 봉사하러 가는 거야.
보미: 뭐라구요? 크리스마스 전날 밤에 자원 봉사를 한다고요? 아빠, 지금 예수님처럼 "네 이웃을 사
랑하라"고 말씀하시는 거예요?
아빠: 보미, 기름 유출이 있었잖니.

아빠는 갑자기 저녁 식사 때 그것을 알리셨다. 우리는 이른 아침에 마을에 도착했다. 많은 사람들이 돌들을 씻어내고 있었다. 우리 가족은 한 팀처럼 일을 했다. 나는 해안에서 몇 마리의 새들을 발견했다. 세리와 나는 한 조로 일을 했다. 우리는 그들의 깃털로부터 기름을 닦아냈다. 우리는 열심히 일했고 식사조차 걸렀다. 하루가 끝날 무렵 마을 사람들은 우리에게 감사를 표시했다. 아빠는 "보미와 세리, 너희들 오늘 정말 열심히 일했구나. 나는 너희가 자랑스럽다"라고 말씀하셨다.

## village
[vílidʒ]
n. 마을

Tomorrow we will leave for an ocean village.
내일 우리는 해안 마을로 떠날 거야.
- villager  마을 사람

## far
[fáːr]
a. 먼

It's far from Seoul.
그곳은 서울에서 멀리 떨어져 있어.

## shower
[ʃáuər]
n. 샤워
v. 샤워하다, 잔뜩 주다

Dad, can we take a shower with hot water?
아빠, 뜨거운 물로 샤워할 수 있나요?
- take a shower  샤워하다

## seafood
[síːfùːd]
n. 해산물

Can we have delicious seafood there?
거기에서 맛있는 해산물을 먹을 수 있나요?

## volunteer
[vàləntíər]
v. 자원 봉사하다
n. 자원자

Bomi, we're going to volunteer there.
보미, 우리는 자원 봉사하러 가는 거야.
- volunteer - volunteered - volunteered

## pardon
[páːrdn]
v. 용서하다
n. 용서

Pardon?
뭐라구요?
- pardon - pardoned - pardoned

## eve
[íːv]
n. 전날 밤

Volunteering on Christmas Eve?
크리스마스 전날 밤에 자원 봉사를 한다고요?

## neighbor
[néibər]
n. 이웃(사람)

Dad, are you talking like Jesus, "Love your neighbors?"
아빠, 지금 예수님처럼 "네 이웃을 사랑하라"고 말씀하시는 거예요?

- neighborhood  n. 이웃, 동네
- neighboring  a. 이웃의, 근접한

## oil spill
[ɔ́il spìl]
기름 유출

Bomi, there was an oil spill.
보미, 기름 유출이 있었잖니.

## announce
[ənáuns]
v. 알리다, 발표하다

Dad announced the news suddenly at dinner.
아빠는 갑자기 저녁 식사 때 그것을 알리셨다.

- announcement  n. 발표, 공고
- announce - announced - announced

## dinner
[dínər]
n. 식사, 정찬

Dad announced the news suddenly at dinner.
아빠는 갑자기 저녁 식사 때 그것을 알리셨다.

## reach
[ríːtʃ]
v. ~에 도착하다

We reached the village in the early morning.
우리는 이른 아침에 마을에 도착했다.

- reachable  a. 닿을 수 있는
- reach - reached - reached

## rinse
[ríns]
v. 씻어내다, 헹구다

Many people were rinsing off rocks.
많은 사람들이 돌들을 씻어내고 있었다.

- rinse - rinsed - rinsed

## team
[tíːm]
n. 단체, 팀  v. 팀을 이루다

Our family worked like a team.
우리 가족은 한 팀처럼 일을 했다.

## coast
[kóust]
n. 해안

I found some birds on the coast.
나는 해안에서 몇 마리의 새들을 발견했다.
- coastal  a. 해안의

## pair
[pɛ́ər]
n. 한 쌍, 2인조

Seri and I did pair work.
세리와 나는 한 조로 일을 했다.

## feather
[féðər]
n. 깃털

We cleaned oil from their feathers.
우리는 그들의 깃털로부터 기름을 닦아냈다.

## meal
[míːl]
n. 식사

We worked hard and even skipped a meal.
우리는 열심히 일했고 식사조차 걸렀다.

## appreciation
[əpriːʃiéiʃən]
n. 감사

At the end of the day, the villagers showed their appreciation to us.
하루가 끝날 무렵에 마을 사람들은 우리에게 감사를 표시했다.
- appreciate  v. 감사하다

## really
[ríːəli]
ad. 정말로, 실제로

Dad said, "Bomi and Seri, you were really hardworking today. I'm proud of you."
아빠는 "보미와 세리, 너희들 오늘 정말 열심히 일했구나. 나는 너희가 자랑스럽다"라고 말씀하셨다.

## hardworking
[háːrdwəːrkiŋ]
a. 열심히 일하는

Dad said, "Bomi and Seri, you were really hardworking today. I'm proud of you."
아빠는 "보미와 세리, 너희들 오늘 정말 열심히 일했구나. 나는 너희가 자랑스럽다"라고 말씀하셨다.

# Check Again!

**A** Translate each word or expression into Korean.

1. reach .................................
2. coast .................................
3. oil spill .................................
4. meal .................................
5. really .................................
6. feather .................................
7. neighbor .................................
8. far .................................
9. pardon .................................
10. rinse .................................

**B** Translate each word or expression into English.

1. 감사 .................................
2. 자원 봉사하다 .................................
3. 해산물 .................................
4. 식사, 정찬 .................................
5. 한 쌍, 2인조 .................................

**C** Fill in the blank with the appropriate word. Refer to the Korean.

1. We decorate a Christmas tree on Christmas E_____ .
   우리는 크리스마스 이브에 크리스마스 트리를 장식한다.

2. The teacher a_____ that there would be no school tomorrow.
   선생님께서는 내일 수업이 없다고 발표하셨다.

3. Sujin took a s_____ before bed.
   수진은 자기 전에 샤워를 했다.

4. I think both of you are really h_____ .
   나는 너희 둘 모두 정말 열심히 일을 한다고 생각해.

5. The v_____ looked weird and spooky.
   그 마을은 이상하고 으스스해 보였다.

# Chapter 9
# Politics and Social Issues

Unit 23. Seri will design school uniforms for girls.

make hair too **firm**

be not allowed to wear **loose** pants

**look** at the handout

like hair **dyed** purple

# Episode

Seri: Let's use my hair **spray**.

Bomi: Hey, you're making my hair too **firm**.

Seri: Bomi, why do you always wear **either** a black or a gray coat? • Why do you wear a **skirt** on cold days?

Bomi: We can't wear **loose** pants at school.

Seri: That's **unfair**. • Someday I will design school **uniforms** for girls.

Bomi: Seri, look at this **handout**. • It's about our school **regulations**.

Seri: You **underlined** some parts. • What's this **rule** for? • **Colorful** coats are not allowed? • Now I understand the **reason**. • That's why you wear such **boring** coats. • Even Sara's pet likes her hair **dyed purple**.

Bomi: Right. I want to **express** my **personality**. • Why aren't **middle** school students **allowed** to do so?

---

세리: 내 헤어 스프레이를 써보자.
보미: 이봐, 너는 내 머리를 너무 단단하게 만들고 있어.
세리: 보미 언니, 왜 언니는 항상 검정 또는 회색 코트만 입어? 왜 추운 날에 치마를 입어?
보미: 우리는 학교에 헐렁한 바지를 입고 갈 수 없어.
세리: 그것은 불공평해. 언젠가 나는 여자아이들을 위한 교복을 디자인할 거야.
보미: 세리, 이 인쇄물을 봐. 우리 학교의 규칙들이야.
세리: 몇몇 부분에 밑줄을 쳤네. 이 규칙은 왜 있는 거야? 다채로운 코트들은 허용이 안 된다고? 이제 이유를 이해하겠네. 그래서 언니는 그렇게 지루한 코트들을 입는구나. 심지어 사라 언니의 애완 동물도 털을 보라색으로 염색하는 걸 좋아해.
보미: 맞아. 나도 나의 개성을 표현하고 싶어. 왜 중학생들은 그렇게 하는 것이 허용이 안 되지?

## spray
[spréi]
n. 스프레이 v. 뿌리다

Let's use my hair spray.
내 헤어 스프레이를 써보자.

## firm
[fə́ːrm]
a. 단단한, 굳은 n. 회사

Hey, you're making my hair too firm.
이봐, 너는 내 머리를 너무 단단하게 만들고 있어.
- firmly  ad. 단단하게

## either
[íːðər]
conj. ~거나 ~거나
a. 둘 중 하나의

Bomi, why do you always wear either a black or a gray coat?
보미, 왜 항상 검정 또는 회색 코트만 입어?
- either A or B  A 또는 B

## skirt
[skə́ːrt]
n. 치마

Why do you wear a skirt on cold days?
왜 추운 날에 치마를 입어?

## loose
[lúːs]
a. 헐렁한

We can't wear loose pants at school.
우리는 학교에 헐렁한 바지를 입고 갈 수 없어.
- loosen  v. 헐렁하게 하다

## unfair
[ʌnfɛ́ər]
a. 불공평한

That's unfair.
그것은 불공평해.
- fair  a. 공평한

## uniform
[júːnəfɔːrm]
n. 제복, 교복

Someday I will design school uniforms for girls.
언젠가 나는 여자아이들을 위한 교복을 디자인할 거야.

## handout
[hǽndàut]
n. 유인물

Seri, look at this handout.
세리, 이 인쇄물을 봐.

## regulation
[règjəléiʃən]
n. 규정

It's about our school regulations.
우리 학교의 규칙들이야.

- regulate  v. 규제하다

## underline
[ʌ̀ndərláin]
v. 밑줄을 긋다  n. 밑줄

You underlined some parts.
몇몇 부분에 밑줄을 쳤네.

- underline - underlined - underlined

## rule
[rúːl]
n. 규칙  v. 지배하다

What's this rule for?
이 규칙은 왜 있는 거야?

## colorful
[kʌ́lərfəl]
a. 다채로운, 화려한

Colorful coats are not allowed?
다채로운 코트들은 허용이 안 된다고?

- color  n. 색

## reason
[ríːzən]
n. 이유  v. 설명하다

Now I understand the reason.
이제 이유를 이해하겠네.

- reasonable  a. 합당한

## boring
[bɔ́ːriŋ]
a. 지루한

That's why you wear such boring coats.
그래서 그렇게 지루한 코트들을 입는구나.

## dye
[dái]
v. 염색하다

Even Sara's pet likes her hair dyed purple.
심지어 사라의 애완 동물도 털을 보라색으로 염색하는 걸 좋아해.
- dyed  a. 염색된  • dye - dyed - dyed

## purple
[pə́ːrpl]
a. 자주빛의, 보라빛의

Even Sara's pet likes her hair dyed purple.
심지어 사라의 애완 동물도 털을 보라색으로 염색하는 걸 좋아해.

## express
[iksprés]
v. 표현하다

Right. I want to express my personality.
맞아. 나는 나의 개성을 표현하고 싶어.
- expression  n. 표현  • expressive  a. 표현적인
- express - expressed - expressed

## personality
[pə̀ːrsənǽləti]
n. 개성

Right. I want to express my personality.
맞아. 나는 나의 개성을 표현하고 싶어.
- express one's personality  개성을 표현하다

## middle
[mídl]
a. 가운데의

Why aren't middle school students allowed to do so?
왜 중학생들은 그렇게 하는 것이 허용이 안 되지?
- middle school  중학교

## allow
[əláu]
v. 허가하다, 허락하다

Why aren't middle school students allowed to do so?
왜 중학생들은 그렇게 하는 것이 허용이 안 되지?
- allowance  n. 허용, 허락
- allow - allowed - allowed

# Check Again!

**A** Translate each word or expression into Korean.

1. handout ........................
2. purple ........................
3. express ........................
4. dye ........................
5. allow ........................
6. middle ........................
7. loose ........................
8. rule ........................
9. underline ........................
10. personality ........................

**B** Translate each word or expression into English.

1. 불공평한 ........................
2. 다채로운 ........................
3. 지루한 ........................
4. 단단한 ........................
5. 제복, 교복 ........................

**C** Fill in the blank with the appropriate word. Refer to the Korean.

1. The r_____ in our dormitory are too strict.
   우리 기숙사의 규정은 너무 엄격하다.

2. A: Which jacket would you like to take? 어떤 재킷을 살 거니?
   B: E_____ the red jacket or the blue one will be fine.
   빨간색이나 파란색이 좋겠어.

3. We can draw attention by using c_____ letters.
   우리는 다채로운 글자를 사용해서 시선을 끌 수 있다.

4. Teens like to e_____ their own personalities.
   10대는 그들의 개성을 표현하고 싶어한다.

5. What was the r_____ you shouted at me?
   네가 나에게 소리친 이유가 뭐였어?

Chapter 9. Politics and Social Issues  **179**

# Chapter 9
# Politics and Social Issues

## Unit 24. We add some lines to a song.

have a **message**

have peace

use more gestures

**no borders** between countries

# Episode

Sara: Bomi, I like this song, **Imagine**. • It has a **message**.
• Why not add some **lines** to it?

Bomi: I **agree**. • Imagine if there was no **war**. • We wouldn't need any **soldiers**.

Sara: But who would **protect** our country?

Bomi: Just imagine if there were no **weapons**.

Sara: Then, we would have **peace**. • There wouldn't be any **borders between** countries.

Bomi: Imagine if there was no **language**.

Sara: We would use more **gestures**. • Imagine if there was no **map**.

Bomi: Then, we wouldn't have **enough knowledge** about the world.

Sara: We wouldn't be able to locate where the **deserts** are.

Bomi: Imagine if there was no **education**. • We would have **difficulty** understanding everything.

---

사라: 보미, 나는 '상상해 봐'라는 이 노래가 좋아. 메시지가 있어. 노래에 가사를 더 추가하는 게 어때?
보미: 동의해. 전쟁이 없다고 상상해 봐. 우리는 군인들이 필요 없을 거야.
사라: 하지만 누가 우리나라를 지키지?
보미: 그냥 무기가 하나도 없다고 상상해 봐.
사라: 그러면 우리는 평화로울 거야. 나라 사이의 국경도 없을 거야.
보미: 언어가 없다고 상상해 봐.
사라: 우리는 몸짓을 더 사용하게 될 거야. 지도가 없다고 상상해 봐.
보미: 그러면 우리는 세상에 대한 충분한 지식이 없을 거야.
사라: 사막이 어디에 있는지 알 수 없을 거야.
보미: 교육이 없다고 상상해 봐. 우리는 모든 것을 이해하는 데 어려움이 있을 거야.

## imagine
[imǽdʒin]
v. 상상하다

Bomi, I like this song, Imagine.
보미, 나는 '상상해 봐'라는 이 노래가 좋아.
- imagination   n. 상상력
- imaginary   a. 상상의
- imagine - imagined - imagined

## message
[mésidʒ]
n. 메시지

It has a message.
메시지가 있어.

## line
[láin]
n. 가사

Why not add some lines to it?
노래에 가사를 더 추가하는 게 어때?

## agree
[əgríː]
v. 동의하다

I agree. 동의해.
- agreement   n. 동의
- agreeable   a. 기분 좋은, 동의하는
- agree - agreed - agreed

## war
[wɔːr]
n. 전쟁

Imagine if there was no war.
전쟁이 없다고 상상해 봐.

## soldier
[sóuldʒər]
n. 군인

We wouldn't need any soldiers.
우리는 군인들이 필요 없을 거야.

## protect
[prətékt]
v. 보호하다, 지키다

But who would protect our country?
하지만 누가 우리나라를 지키지?
- protection   n. 보호
- protective   a. 보호하는
- protect - protected - protected

## weapon
[wépən]
n. 무기

Just imagine if there were no weapons.
그냥 무기가 하나도 없다고 상상해 봐.
- weaponize   v. 무기화하다

## peace
[píːs]
n. 평화

Then, we would have peace.
그러면 우리는 평화로울 거야.
- peaceful   a. 평온한

## border
[bɔ́ːrdər]
n. 국경

There wouldn't be any borders between countries.
나라 사이의 국경도 없을 거야.

## between
[bitwíːn]
prep. ~사이에

There wouldn't be any borders between countries.
나라 사이의 국경도 없을 거야.

## language
[lǽŋgwidʒ]
n. 언어

Imagine if there was no language.
언어가 없다고 상상해 봐.

## gesture
[dʒéstʃər]
n. 몸짓

We would use more gestures.
우리는 몸짓을 더 사용하게 될 거야.

## map
[mǽp]
n. 지도

Imagine if there was no map.
지도가 없다고 상상해 봐.

## enough
[ináf]
a. 충분한

Then, we wouldn't have enough knowledge about the world.
그러면 우리는 세상에 대한 충분한 지식이 없을 거야.

## knowledge
[nάlidʒ]
n. 지식

Then, we wouldn't have enough knowledge about the world.
그러면 우리는 세상에 대한 충분한 지식이 없을 거야.

- knowledgeable　a. 지식 있는, 식견이 있는

## desert
[dézəːrt]
n. 사막　a. 사막 같은, 불모의
v. 버리다

We wouldn't be able to locate where the deserts are.
사막이 어디에 있는지 알 수 없을 거야.

## education
[èdʒukéiʃən]
n. 교육

Imagine if there was no education.
교육이 없다고 상상해 봐.

- educational　a. 교육적인

## difficulty
[dífikʌlti]
n. 어려움

We would have difficulty understanding everything.
우리는 모든 것을 이해하는 데 어려움이 있을 거야.

- difficult　a. 어려운
- have difficulty ~ing　~하는 데 어려움을 겪다

# Check Again!

**A** Translate each word or expression into Korean.

1. map .....................
2. knowledge .....................
3. enough .....................
4. desert .....................
5. war .....................
6. soldier .....................
7. imagine .....................
8. message .....................
9. between .....................
10. line .....................

**B** Translate each word or expression into English.

1. 무기 .....................
2. 평화 .....................
3. 교육 .....................
4. 언어 .....................
5. 국경 .....................

**C** Fill in the blank with the appropriate word. Refer to the Korean.

1. Finally he a_____ with us.
   드디어 그는 우리에게 동의를 했어.

2. Do you think English e_____ is hard to get in Korea?
   한국에서 영어 교육을 받기 어렵다고 생각하세요?

3. G_____ mean different things from country to country.
   몸짓은 나라마다 그 의미가 다르다.

4. They had d_____ finding Susan's place.
   그들은 수잔의 집을 찾느라 어려움을 겪었다.

5. My sisters always p_____ me from danger.
   나의 언니들은 항상 나를 위험으로부터 보호해 준다.

Chapter 9. Politics and Social Issues   **185**

# At a park

1. ride a bike 자전거 타다
2. make loud noises 소음을 내다
3. throw trash 쓰레기를 버리다
4. cover one's ears 귀를 막다
5. walk one's dog 개를 산책시키다
6. pick flowers 꽃을 꺾다

- **Don't rollerblade** without a helmet.
  헬멧을 쓰지 않은 채 롤러블레이드를 타지 마세요.

- **Don't make loud noises.**
  큰 소음을 내지 마세요.

- **Don't pick flowers.**
  꽃을 꺾지 마세요.

- **Don't throw trash.**
  쓰레기를 버리지 마세요.

- **Don't walk your dog** along the path. It's for pedestrians only.
  도로에서 개를 산책시키지 마세요. 보행자 전용이에요.

- **Don't ride a bike** along the path. It's for pedestrians only.
  도로에서 자전거를 타지 마세요. 보행자 전용이에요.

*Culture Plus*

### Environment 환경

+ pollution 오염
+ water pollution 수질 오염
+ air pollution 공기 오염
+ oil spill 기름 유출
+ disposable 일회용품
+ plastic bag 비닐봉지
+ recycling 재활용
+ recycling bin 재활용 통

# STORYTELLING VOCABULARY

## GREEN

## Chapter 10. Economy

**Unit 25.** We discuss how to save money.
**Unit 26.** Good job, Brownie!
**Unit 27.** Sorry, Seri!

# Chapter 10
# Economy

Unit 25. We discuss how to save money.

**talk on** the wireless **phone**

**go shopping**

**use** store **coupons**

**unplug things**

# Episode

D a d: Let's discuss how we can **save money**.

Bomi: I have a good **example**. • Seri, don't talk so long on the **wireless** phone.

S e r i: Ha! Don't **chat** so long on your cell phone, Bomi!

D a d: And when should we make **international** calls?

Bomi: Late at **night**. • They are **cheaper** then.

Mom: And I'll try to **go shopping** in the late afternoon. • **Goods** are cheaper then.

S e r i: And go to the **outdoor market**, right?

Mom: Yes. Goods are cheaper there than at the **department stores**. • But make use of department store **sales**.

Bomi: I always try to use store **coupons**.

Hoony: I know how to save **electricity**. • **Turn** off **lights**. • And **unplug** things when they're not in use.

Mom: Wow, you are all so **wise** about saving money!

아빠: 돈을 절약할 수 있는 방법에 대해 의논하자.
보미: 제게 좋은 예가 떠올랐어요. 세리, 무선 전화기로 오래 통화하지 마.
세리: 하! 보미 언니는 휴대 전화로 오래 수다 떨지 마!
아빠: 그리고 국제 전화는 언제 하는 것이 좋지?
보미: 밤 늦게요. 그때 요금이 더 싸요.
엄마: 그리고 나는 오후 늦게 장보러 가려고 해. 물건이 그때 더 싸거든.
세리: 그리고 재래시장으로 가야죠, 그렇죠?
엄마: 그래. 그곳 물건이 백화점에서보다 더 싸단다. 하지만 백화점 세일을 활용해야지.
보미: 저는 항상 가게 쿠폰을 이용하려고 해요.
후니: 저는 전기를 아끼는 방법을 알아요. 불을 꺼요. 그리고 사용하지 않을 때는 플러그를 빼요.
엄마: 와, 너희 모두 돈을 절약하는 방법에 대해 잘 알고 있구나!

## save
[séiv]
v. 절약하다, 아끼다

Let's discuss how we can save money.
돈을 절약할 수 있는 방법에 대해 의논하자.
- saving   n. 절약   a. 절약하는
- save - saved - saved

## money
[mʌ́ni]
n. 돈, 화폐

Let's discuss how we can save money.
돈을 절약할 수 있는 방법에 대해 의논하자.

## example
[igzǽmpəl]
n. 보기, 예

I have a good example.
제게 좋은 예가 떠올랐어요.

## wireless
[wáiərlis]
a. 무선의

Seri, don't talk so long on the wireless phone.
세리, 무선 전화기로 오래 통화하지 마.
- wire   n. 전선, 전화선

## chat
[tʃæt]
v. 수다를 떨다   n. 잡담, 담소

Ha! Don't chat so long on your cell phone, Bomi!
하! 보미, 휴대 전화로 오래 수다 떨지 마!
- chat - chatted - chatted

## international
[intərnǽʃənəl]
a. 국제적인, 국제간의

And when should we make international calls?
그리고 국제 전화는 언제 하는 것이 좋지?
- make an international call   국제 전화하다

## night
[nàit]
n. 밤

Late at night.
밤 늦게요.

## cheaper
[tʃíːpər]
a. 값이 더 싼

They are cheaper then.
그것은 그때 더 싸요.
- cheap  a. 값이 싼  • cheapest  a. 값이 가장 싼

## shopping
[ʃápiŋ]
n. 쇼핑, 물건 사기, 장보기

And I'll try to go shopping in the late afternoon.
그리고 나는 오후 늦게 장보러 가려고 해.
- go shopping  쇼핑하러 가다, 장보러 가다

## goods
[gúdz]
n. 상품, 물품

Goods are cheaper then.
물건이 그때 더 싸거든.

## outdoor
[áutdɔ̀ːr]
a. 야외의

And go to the outdoor market, right?
그리고 재래시장에 가야죠, 그렇죠?

## market
[máːrkit]
n. 시장

And go to the outdoor market, right?
그리고 재래시장에 가야죠, 그렇죠?
- outdoor market  n. 재래시장

## department store
[dipáːrtmənt stɔ̀ːr]
백화점

Yes. Goods are cheaper there than at the department stores.
그래. 그곳 물건이 백화점에서보다 더 싸단다.

## sale
[séil]
n. 세일, 할인행사

But make use of department store sales.
하지만 백화점 세일을 활용해야지.

## coupon
[kjúːpɑn]
n. 쿠폰, 할인권

I always try to use store coupons.
저는 항상 가게 쿠폰을 이용하려고 해요.

## electricity
[ilèktrísəti]
n. 전기

I know how to save electricity.
저는 전기를 아끼는 방법을 알아요.

## turn
[tə́ːrn]
v. 돌리다

Turn off lights.
불을 꺼요.

- turn off (불, 전등 등을) 끄다
- turn on (불, 전등 등을) 켜다
- turn - turned - turned

## light
[làit]
n. 빛, 등불

Turn off lights.
불을 꺼요.

## unplug
[ʌ̀nplʌ́g]
v. 플러그를 뽑다

And unplug things when they're not in use.
그리고 사용하지 않을 때는 플러그를 빼요.

- plug in v. 플러그를 꽂다 · plug n. 플러그
- unplug - unplugged - unplugged

## wise
[wáiz]
a. 현명한, 박식한

Wow, you are all so wise about saving money!
와, 너희 모두 돈을 절약하는 방법에 대해 잘 알고 있구나!

- wisdom n. 지혜

# Check Again!

**A** Translate each word or expression into Korean.

1. example ................................
2. international ................................
3. cheaper ................................
4. outdoor ................................
5. market ................................
6. department store ................................
7. coupon ................................
8. electricity ................................
9. wireless ................................
10. unplug ................................

**B** Translate each word or expression into English.

1. 절약하다 ................................
2. 수다를 떨다 ................................
3. 상품, 물품 ................................
4. 할인행사 ................................
5. 현명한 ................................

**C** Fill in the blank with the appropriate word. Refer to the Korean.

1. Who could be calling so late at n_____?
   누가 이렇게 밤 늦게 전화를 거는 걸까요?

2. The guide gave us some time to go s_____.
   가이드가 우리에게 쇼핑하러 갈 시간을 주었다.

3. Using less hot water will help s_____ money on gas.
   뜨거운 물을 덜 쓰면 가스 비용을 줄이는 데 도움이 될 겁니다.

4. I had a real honest c_____ with my mom.
   나는 엄마와 아주 솔직한 담화를 나누었어요.

5. Please t_____ off all your cell phones during the show.
   공연 동안 휴대 전화를 모두 꺼주세요.

# Chapter 10
# Economy

### Unit 26. Good job, Brownie!

ride a skateboard

get prize money

hate standing on the skateboard

have something as a reward

# Episode

Bomi: I can't buy a **ticket** to the Volcanoes' **concert**. • I can't **spend** over 50,000 won on it.

Sara: I can't **afford** one, either. • They are so **expensive**!

Bomi: Hey, look at that **ad**. • That dog is riding a **skateboard**.

Sara: It says they are picking new **models**. • The winners get **prize** money. • We should **enter** Brownie!

Bomi: Yes, let's get her to **pose** on this skateboard.

Sara: Put these **sunglasses** on her. • Good. I'll take her **photograph**.

Bomi: Ugh! Brownie **hates standing** on the skateboard. • Calm down, Brownie. • I don't want to **anger** you. • I'm **begging** you, Brownie!

Sara: Yes, I finally got it! • **Excellent**, Brownie!

Bomi: Great, we **succeeded**! • Good **job**, Brownie!

Sara: Here, have some tuna as a **reward**.

Bomi: Have some milk, Brownie. • You look **thirsty**.

보미: 나는 볼케이노 콘서트 티켓을 살 수 없어. 나는 티켓에 5만원 이상 쓸 수 없어.
사라: 나도 표를 살 돈이 안돼. 티켓이 너무 비싸!
보미: 저기, 저 광고 좀 봐. 저 개가 스케이트보드를 타고 있어.
사라: 새로운 모델을 뽑고 있다고 하네. 우승자들에게 상금을 준대. 우리 브라우니를 참가시키자!
보미: 그래, 브라우니가 이 스케이트보드 위에 포즈를 취하게 하자.
사라: 브라우니에게 이 선글라스를 씌워 봐. 좋아, 내가 사진을 찍을게.
보미: 아이! 브라우니가 스케이트보드 위에 서 있는 것을 몹시 싫어해. 진정해, 브라우니. 너를 화나게 하고 싶지 않아. 이렇게 빌게, 브라우니!
사라: 그래, 드디어 찍었어! 잘했어, 브라우니!
보미: 잘됐다, 우리가 해낸 거야! 수고했어, 브라우니!
사라: 자 여기, 상으로 참치 좀 먹어.
보미: 우유 먹어, 브라우니. 목말라 보여.

## ticket
[tíkit]
n. 표, 입장권

I can't buy a ticket to the Volcanoes' concert.
나는 볼케이노 콘서트 티켓을 살 수 없어.

## concert
[kánsə:rt]
n. 콘서트, 음악회

I can't buy a ticket to the Volcanoes' concert.
나는 볼케이노 콘서트 티켓을 살 수 없어.

## spend
[spénd]
v. 쓰다, 소비하다
n. 지출, 비용

I can't spend over 50,000 won on it.
나는 그것에 5만원 이상 쓸 수 없어.

- spend - spent - spent

## afford
[əfɔ́:rd]
v. ~할 여유가 있다

I can't afford one, either.
나도 표를 살 돈이 안돼.

- affordable  a. 줄 수 있는, (가격이) 알맞은
- afford - afforded - afforded

## expensive
[ikspénsiv]
a. 비싼

They are so expensive!
너무 비싸!

## ad
[ǽd]
n. 광고
(advertisement의 줄임말)

Hey, look at that ad.
저기, 저 광고 좀 봐.

## skateboard
[skéitbɔ̀:rd]
n. 스케이트보드

That dog is riding a skateboard.
저 개가 스케이트보드를 타고 있어.

## model
[mádl]
n. 모델

It says they are picking new models.
새로운 모델을 뽑고 있다고 하네.

### prize
[práiz]
n. 상, 포상

The winners get prize money.
우승자들에게 상금을 준다.
- prize money  상금

### enter
[éntər]
v. (경기 등에) 참가시키다

We should enter Brownie!
우리 브라우니를 참가시키자!
- enter - entered - entered

### pose
[póuz]
v. 자세(포즈)를 취하다
n. 자세(포즈)

Yes, let's get her to pose on this skateboard.
그래, 브라우니가 이 스케이트보드 위에 포즈를 취하게 하자.
- pose - posed - posed

### sunglasses
[sʌ́nglæ̀siz]
n. 선글라스

Put these sunglasses on her.
이 선글라스를 씌워 봐.

### photograph
[fóutəgræ̀f]
n. 사진  v. 사진을 찍다

Good. I'll take her photograph.
좋아, 내가 사진을 찍을게.
- take a photograph  사진을 찍다

### hate
[héit]
v. 몹시 싫어하다

Ugh! Brownie hates standing on the skateboard.
아이! 브라우니가 스케이트보드 위에 서 있는 것을 몹시 싫어해.
- hatred  n. 증오, 미움
- hate - hated - hated

### stand
[stǽnd]
v. 서다, 일어서다

Ugh! Brownie hates standing on the skateboard.
아이! 브라우니가 스케이트보드 위에 서 있는 것을 몹시 싫어해.
- stand - stood - stood

## anger
[ǽŋgər]
v. 화나게 하다
n. 노여움, 화

Calm down, Brownie. I don't want to anger you.
진정해, 브라우니. 너를 화나게 하고 싶지 않아.
- anger - angered - angered

## beg
[bég]
v. 빌다, 간청하다

I'm begging you, Brownie!
이렇게 빌게, 브라우니!
- beg - begged - begged

## excellent
[éksələnt]
a. 훌륭한

Excellent, Brownie!
잘했어, 브라우니!
- excellence  n. 우수, 훌륭함

## succeed
[səksíːd]
v. 성공하다

Great, we succeeded!
잘됐다, 우리가 해낸 거야!
- success  n. 성공
- succeed - succeeded - succeeded

## job
[dʒáb]
n. 임무 완수, 역할

Good job, Brownie!
수고했어, 브라우니!

## reward
[riwɔ́ːrd]
n. 보수, 보상

Here, have some tuna as a reward.
자 여기, 상으로 참치 좀 먹어.
- rewardless  a. 무보수의, 헛수고의

## thirsty
[θə́ːrsti]
a. 목마른, 갈망하는

Have some milk, Brownie. You look thirsty.
우유 먹어, 브라우니. 목말라 보여.
- thirst  n. 갈증

# Check Again!

**A** Translate each word or expression into Korean.

1. afford .................................
2. expensive .................................
3. prize .................................
4. enter .................................
5. photograph .................................
6. beg .................................
7. stand .................................
8. excellent .................................
9. succeed .................................
10. spend .................................

**B** Translate each word or expression into English.

1. 표, 입장권 .................................
2. 광고 .................................
3. 몹시 싫어하다 .................................
4. 임무 완수 .................................
5. 목마른 .................................

**C** Fill in the blank with the appropriate word. Refer to the Korean.

1. Harry jumped in the air then got back on his s_____.
   해리는 공중에서 뛴 다음 다시 스케이트보드에 탔습니다.

2. She is now a m_____ for their notebook computer.
   그녀는 이제 그 회사 노트북 컴퓨터의 모델이에요.

3. It was hard to p_____ in a pyramid.
   피라미드를 만들어 포즈를 취하기가 힘들었어요.

4. Why do some people wear s_____ indoors?
   왜 어떤 사람들은 실내에서 선글라스를 쓰죠?

5. He got some money as a r_____.
   그는 보상으로 돈을 받았다.

# Chapter 10
# Economy

Unit 27. Sorry, Seri!

take a deep breath

catch everyone's attention

can't find a thief

fit someone perfectly

# Episode

Dear Seri,

You look so **cute** today, Seri. • You're such a **warm-hearted** person. • Please take a **deep breath** and listen to me. • You know your **brand-new** MP3 player? • Well, I **borrowed** it and took it to school. • It caught everyone's **attention**. • My classmates thought it was really **cool**. • But when I **returned** from PE class it wasn't in my bag. • Someone **stole** it! • We couldn't find the **thief**. • Oh, I should have listened to mom's **advice**. • She said I should **leave** it at home. • Look, my **favorite** jacket is yours. • It will **fit** you perfectly. • It was a **bit tight** for me **anyway**. • It's a really **famous** brand. • It's perfect **except** that it's two years old. • So take it and please **forgive** me!

---

세리에게,

너 오늘 정말 귀엽다, 세리. 너는 정말로 마음이 따뜻한 사람이야. 제발 숨을 크게 쉬고 내 말을 좀 들어줘. 너의 새 MP3 플레이어 있잖아? 음, 내가 그걸 빌려서 학교에 가져갔었어. 모든 애들의 시선을 사로잡았어. 같은 반 애들은 그게 아주 멋지다고 생각했어. 그런데 체육 시간이 끝나고 돌아오니 그것이 내 가방 안에 없었어. 누군가가 훔쳐갔어! 우리는 도둑을 못 찾았어. 아, 나는 엄마의 조언을 들었어야 했어. 엄마는 그걸 집에 두고 가는 게 좋겠다고 하셨거든. 이봐, 내가 좋아하는 재킷이 이제 네 거야. 너에게 딱 맞을 거야. 어차피 나에게는 조금 끼었거든. 그건 아주 유명한 브랜드야. 2년 정도 되었다는 것을 제외하면 완벽해. 그러니 그것을 갖고 제발 나를 용서해 줘!

## cute
[kjú:t]
a. 귀여운, 예쁜

You look so cute today, Seri.
너 오늘 정말 귀엽다, 세리.

## warm-hearted
[wɔ́:rmhá:rtid]
a. 인정이 있는, 친절한

You're such a warm-hearted person.
너는 정말로 마음이 따뜻한 사람이야.

## deep
[dí:p]
a. 깊은

Please take a deep breath and listen to me.
제발 숨을 크게 쉬고 내 말을 좀 들어줘.
- depth  n. 깊이

## breath
[bréθ]
n. 숨, 호흡

Please take a deep breath and listen to me.
제발 숨을 크게 쉬고 내 말을 좀 들어줘.
- breathe  v. 숨쉬다 • take a breath  숨을 쉬다

## brand-new
[brǽndnjù:]
a. 아주 새로운, 신품의

You know your brand-new MP3 player?
너의 새 MP3 플레이어 있잖아?

## borrow
[bɔ́(:)rou]
v. 빌리다

Well, I borrowed it and took it to school.
음, 내가 그걸 빌려서 학교에 가져갔었어.
- lend  v. 빌려주다
- borrow - borrowed - borrowed

## attention
[əténʃən]
n. 주의, 주목

It caught everyone's attention.
모든 애들의 시선을 사로잡았어.
- attentive  a. 주의 깊은, 경청하는
- catch one's attention  ~의 주의를 끌다

## cool
[kúːl]
a. 멋진, 시원한

My classmates thought it was really cool.
같은 반 애들은 그게 아주 멋지다고 생각했어.

## return
[ritə́ːrn]
v. 되돌아오다(가다)

But when I returned from PE class it wasn't in my bag.
그런데 체육 시간이 끝나고 돌아오니 그것이 내 가방 안에 없었어.

- return - returned - returned

## steal
[stíːl]
v. 훔치다

Someone stole it!
누군가가 훔쳐갔어!

- stolen  a. 훔친  • steal - stole - stolen

## thief
[θíːf]
n. 도둑

We couldn't find the thief.
우리는 도둑을 못 찾았어.

## advice
[ædváis]
n. 조언, 충고

Oh, I should have listened to mom's advice.
아, 나는 엄마의 조언을 들었어야 했어.

- advise  v. 조언하다

## leave
[líːv]
v. 남기다, 두고 가다(오다)

She said I should leave it at home.
그녀는 그걸 집에 두고 가는 게 좋겠다고 하셨거든.

- leave - left - left

## favorite
[féivərit]
a. 좋아하는

Look, my favorite jacket is yours.
이봐, 내가 좋아하는 재킷이 이제 네 거야.

Chapter 10. Economy  **205**

## fit
[fít]
v. ~에 꼭 맞다, 어울리다

It will fit you perfectly.
너에게 딱 맞을 거야.
- fitness  n. 적합, 적성, 건강함
- fit - fitted - fitted

## bit
[bít]
n. 조각, 조금

It was a bit tight for me anyway.
어차피 나에게는 조금 끼었거든.
- a bit  n. 조금, 약간

## tight
[táit]
a. 꼭 끼는

It was a bit tight for me anyway.
어차피 나에게는 조금 끼었거든.
- tighten  v. 죄다, 조이다

## anyway
[éniwèi]
ad. 어쨌든, 아무튼

It was a bit tight for me anyway.
어차피 나에게는 조금 끼었거든.

## famous
[féiməs]
a. 유명한

It's a really famous brand.
그건 아주 유명한 브랜드야.
- fame  n. 명성

## except
[iksépt]
conj. ~를 제외하고
prep. ~외에는

It's perfect except that it's two years old.
2년 정도 되었다는 것을 제외하면 완벽해.
- exception  n. 예외

## forgive
[fərgív]
v. 용서하다

So take it and please forgive me!
그러니 그것을 갖고 제발 나를 용서해 줘!
- forgiveness  n. 용서, 관용
- forgive - forgave - forgiven

# Check Again!

**A** Translate each word or expression into Korean.

1. warm-hearted ...........................
2. cool ...........................
3. borrow ...........................
4. famous ...........................
5. return ...........................
6. steal ...........................
7. anyway ...........................
8. advice ...........................
9. favorite ...........................
10. forgive ...........................

**B** Translate each word or expression into English.

1. 귀여운 ...........................
2. 아주 새로운 ...........................
3. 깊은 ...........................
4. 남겨두다 ...........................
5. 꼭 끼는 ...........................

**C** Fill in the blank with the appropriate word. Refer to the Korean.

1. The movie star caught people's a_____ .
   그 영화배우는 사람들의 관심을 끌었다.

2. Now take a deep b_____ .
   이제 숨을 크게 들이쉬어.

3. She gave me some good a_____ about love.
   그녀는 내게 사랑에 대해 좋은 조언을 해주었어요.

4. I got everything we need e_____ the drinks.
   나는 음료수만 빼고는 우리가 필요한 것을 다 구했어요.

5. My clothes should probably f_____ you nicely.
   내 옷이 아마 너에게 잘 맞을 거야.

# At a supermarket

1. cashier 출납계원
2. shopper 쇼핑하는 사람
3. counter 계산대
4. credit card 신용카드
5. shopping list 쇼핑 리스트
6. shopping cart 쇼핑 카트
7. express lane 빠른 계산대
8. receipt 영수증
9. parcel 꾸러미

- I **check my shopping list**.
  나는 내 쇼핑 리스트를 확인해요.

- I **pack my parcel**.
  나는 내 짐을 포장해요.

- I **use my credit card**.
  나는 신용카드를 사용해요.

- I **use the express lane** for a few items.
  나는 몇 개 안 되는 품목인 경우에 빠른 계산대를 이용해요.

- I **check for the sale items**.
  나는 세일 품목을 확인해요.

- I **use a shopping cart**.
  나는 쇼핑 카트를 사용해요.

- I **get a receipt** from a cashier.
  나는 출납계원으로부터 영수증을 받아요.

### Culture Plus

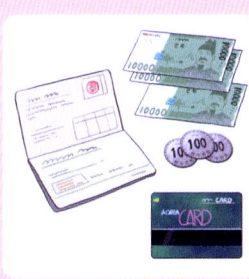

**At a bank** 은행에서

- +bank book  통장
- +credit card  신용카드
- +ATM  현금 자동 인출기
- +bank teller  은행 직원
- +cash  현금
- +coin  동전
- +bill  지폐
- +check  수표

# STORYTELLING VOCABULARY

## GREEN

## Chapter 11. Technology

**Unit 28.** Sara and I are at a robot contest.

**Unit 29.** Grandma belongs to the Internet fishing community.

# Chapter 11
# Technology

Unit 28. Sara and I are at a robot contest.

**bend** one's legs

**serve food**

**invite** friends over

# Episode

Dear Diary,

Sara and I left to go **downtown**. • Now, we are at the robot **contest**. • Wow, robots can do **plenty** of **things**. • Some robots even **carry furniture**.

Sara: Look at that robot. • It's **greeting** people! • It can **bend** its legs.
Bomi: I like its gentle **smile**.
Sara: The robot is counting **sheets** of paper.
Bomi: Hey, the robot over there is **serving** food. • And the robot beside it is **mixing** something. • I can see it mixing **flour** and eggs.
Sara: It looks more like a human than a **machine**. • The inventors must be **geniuses**.
Bomi: I want to have a **compact** robot. • I don't want it to be **heavy**. • I will **invite** friends over more **often** if it helps me with cleaning.
Sara: The robot has to be **clever**. • I want it to **drive** us to school.

---

다이어리에게,
사라와 나는 시내에 갔어. 지금 우리는 로봇 콘테스트에 와 있어. 와, 로봇은 많은 것들을 할 수 있어. 몇몇 로봇들은 심지어 가구도 운반할 수 있어.

사라: 저 로봇 봐. 사람들에게 인사하고 있어! 다리도 구부릴 수 있어.
보미: 나는 그 로봇의 친절한 미소가 좋아.
사라: 로봇이 종이의 장 수를 세고 있어.
보미: 이봐, 저기 있는 로봇은 음식을 내고 있어. 그리고 그 옆에 있는 로봇은 무엇인가를 섞고 있어. 밀가루와 계란을 섞고 있어.
사라: 기계보다는 사람처럼 생겼어. 그 발명가들은 천재들임에 틀림이 없어.
보미: 나는 아담한 로봇을 원해. 무겁지 않았으면 좋겠어. 그것이 청소를 도와준다면 나는 친구들을 더 자주 초대할 거야.
사라: 그 로봇은 똑똑해야겠네. 나는 그 로봇이 우리를 학교까지 운전해서 데려다 줄 수 있으면 좋겠어.

## downtown
[dáuntàun]
ad. 도심지로
n. 시내, 도심지

Sara and I left to go downtown.
사라와 나는 시내에 갔어.

## contest
[kántest]
n. 대회, 경연, 콘테스트

Now, we are at the robot contest.
지금 우리는 로봇 콘테스트에 와 있어.

## plenty
[plénti]
n. 많음  a. 많은

Wow, robots can do plenty of things.
와, 로봇은 많은 것들을 할 수 있어.
- plentiful  a. 많은  • plenty of  많은

## thing
[θíŋ]
n. 물건, 것

Wow, robots can do plenty of things.
와, 로봇은 많은 것들을 할 수 있어.

## carry
[kǽri]
v. 나르다, 운반하다

Some robots even carry furniture.
몇몇 로봇들은 심지어 가구도 운반할 수 있어.
- carry - carried - carried

## furniture
[fə́ːrnitʃər]
n. 가구

Some robots even carry furniture.
몇몇 로봇들은 심지어 가구도 운반할 수 있어.

## greet
[gríːt]
v. 인사하다

Look at that robot. It's greeting people!
저 로봇 봐. 사람들에게 인사하고 있어!
- greeting  n. 인사
- greet - greeted - greeted

## bend
[bénd]
v. 구부리다

It can bend its legs.
다리도 구부릴 수 있어.
- bendable   a. 구부릴 수 있는
- bend - bent - bent

## smile
[smáil]
n. 미소   v. 미소 짓다

I like its gentle smile.
나는 그 친절한 미소가 좋아.
- smiling   a. 미소 짓는

## sheet
[ʃiːt]
n. 한 장, 시트

The robot is counting sheets of paper.
로봇이 종이의 장 수를 세고 있어.

## serve
[səːrv]
v. 음식을 내다, 음식 시중을 들다

Hey, the robot over there is serving food.
이봐, 저기 있는 로봇은 음식을 내고 있어.
- service   n. 봉사
- serve - served - served

## mix
[míks]
v. 혼합하다, 섞다

And the robot beside it is mixing something.
그리고 그 옆에 있는 로봇은 무엇인가를 섞고 있어.
- mixture   n. 혼합
- mix - mixed - mixed

## flour
[fláuər]
n. 밀가루

I can see it mixing flour and eggs.
밀가루와 계란을 섞고 있어.

## machine
[məʃíːn]
n. 기계

It looks more like a human than a machine.
기계보다는 사람처럼 생겼어.

## genius
[dʒíːnjəs]
n. 천재

The inventors must be geniuses.
그 발명가들은 천재들임에 틀림이 없어.

## compact
[kəmpǽkt]
a. 아담한

I want to have a compact robot.
나는 아담한 로봇을 원해.

## heavy
[hévi]
a. 무거운

I don't want it to be heavy.
무겁지 않았으면 좋겠어.
- heavily  ad. 무겁게

## invite
[inváit]
v. 초대하다

I will invite friends over more often if it helps me with cleaning.
그것이 청소를 도와준다면 나는 친구들을 더 자주 초대할 거야.
- invitation  n. 초대
- invite - invited - invited

## often
[ɔ́ːfən]
ad. 자주, 종종

I will invite friends over more often if it helps me with cleaning.
그것이 청소를 도와준다면 나는 친구들을 더 자주 초대할 거야.

## clever
[klévər]
a. 영리한, 똑똑한

The robot has to be clever.
그 로봇은 똑똑해야겠네.

## drive
[dráiv]
v. 운전하다  n. 드라이브

I want it to drive us to school.
나는 그것이 우리를 학교까지 운전해서 데려다 줄 수 있으면 좋겠어.
- driver  n. 운전사
- drive - drove - driven

# Check Again!

**A** Translate each word or expression into Korean.

1. machine ........................
2. sheet ........................
3. genius ........................
4. furniture ........................
5. mix ........................
6. drive ........................
7. bend ........................
8. invite ........................
9. often ........................
10. heavy ........................

**B** Translate each word or expression into English.

1. 아담한 ........................
2. 인사하다 ........................
3. 나르다, 운반하다 ........................
4. 음식을 내다 ........................
5. 영리한 ........................

**C** Fill in the blank with the appropriate word. Refer to the Korean.

1. The girl spoke to the teacher with a big s_____ .
   그 소녀는 미소를 활짝 지으며 선생님에게 말했다.

2. They added some butter and f_____ to bake cookies.
   그들은 쿠키를 굽기 위해서 밀가루와 버터를 넣었다.

3. My neighbor seems shy whenever I g_____ her.
   나의 이웃은 내가 인사할 때마다 쑥스러워하는 듯하다.

4. Why did you go d_____ with Jason last night?
   어젯밤에 제이슨하고 왜 시내에 갔니?

5. There were p_____ of gifts to share.
   나눌 수 있을 만큼 많은 선물들이 있었다.

# Chapter 11
# Technology

Unit 29. Grandma belongs to the Internet fishing community.

**enjoy** modern **technology**

**cheer** someone **up**

**take pictures** with a cell phone

**go fishing** on an island

# Episode

Dear Diary,
My grandma really enjoys **modern technology**. • Last year mom couldn't attend my **graduation**. • So grandma tried to **cheer** me up. • She said "Cheese" and took **pictures** of me during the **ceremony**.

Grandma: Bomi, it's really **convenient** to take pictures with my cell phone.
Bomi: It's wonderful that you enjoy modern **culture**.
Grandma: I want to **rent** a computer. • I can't send messages to my community **members**.
Bomi: Grandma, what's the **matter** with your computer?
Grandma: I called a **repair** person because it's broken.
Bomi: You can use a computer at the **library**. • By the way, grandma, you're becoming more **sociable**. • Do you **belong** to the Internet fishing community?
Grandma: Yeah, I **joined** it **last** month. • You know, grandpa and I like **fishing**.
Bomi: Then, you're a member of the fishing community. • Do you get a lot of **information** about fishing?
Grandma: Sure. Grandpa and I are going to go fishing on an **island** next month with the members.
Bomi: You two are **full** of energy.

다이어리에게,
우리 할머니는 정말로 현대 기술을 즐기셔. 작년에 엄마가 나의 졸업식에 참석하지 못하셨어. 그래서 할머니는 나를 기분 좋게 하려고 노력하셨어. 졸업식을 하는 동안 할머니께서는 치즈라고 말씀하시면서 나의 사진을 찍으셨어.

할머니: 보미, 내 휴대 전화로 사진 찍는 것이 정말 편리하구나.
보  미: 할머니가 현대 문명을 즐기시니 정말 멋져요.
할머니: 나는 컴퓨터를 대여하고 싶어. 나는 동호회 회원들에게 메시지를 보낼 수가 없어.
보  미: 할머니, 컴퓨터에 무슨 문제가 있나요?
할머니: 그것이 고장이 나서 정비사를 불렀어.
보  미: 도서관에서 컴퓨터 사용하실 수 있으세요. 그런데, 할머니, 점점 더 사교적으로 변하시네요. 인터넷 낚시 동호회 소속이세요?
할머니: 그럼, 지난달에 가입했어. 너도 알다시피 할아버지와 나는 낚시를 좋아해.
보  미: 그럼 할머니는 낚시 동호회 회원이네요. 낚시에 관한 정보도 많이 얻나요?
할머니: 물론이지. 할아버지와 나는 회원들하고 다음 달에 섬으로 낚시를 갈 거야.
보  미: 두 분은 정말 에너지가 넘치세요.

| | |
|---|---|
| **modern**<br>[mάdərn]<br>a. 현대의 | My grandma really enjoys modern technology.<br>우리 할머니는 정말로 현대 기술을 즐기셔. |
| **technology**<br>[teknάlədʒi]<br>n. 기술 | My grandma really enjoys modern technology.<br>우리 할머니는 정말로 현대 기술을 즐기셔. |
| **graduation**<br>[grӕdʒuéiʃən]<br>n. 졸업 | Last year mom couldn't attend my graduation.<br>작년에 엄마가 나의 졸업식에 참석하지 못하셨어.<br>• graduate  v. 졸업하다 |
| **cheer**<br>[tʃíər]<br>v. 격려하다  n. 격려, 환호 | So grandma tried to cheer me up.<br>그래서 할머니는 나를 기분 좋게 하려고 노력하셨어.<br>• cheerful  a. 쾌활한, 기분 좋은<br>• cheer up  기운이 나게 하다, 기분 좋게 하다<br>• cheer - cheered - cheered |
| **picture**<br>[píktʃər]<br>n. 사진 | She said "Cheese" and took pictures of me during the ceremony.<br>졸업식을 하는 동안 그녀는 '치즈'라고 말씀하시면서 나의 사진을 찍으셨어.<br>• take a picture  사진을 찍다 |
| **ceremony**<br>[sérəmòuni]<br>n. 식, 의식 | She said "Cheese" and took pictures of me during the ceremony.<br>졸업식을 하는 동안 그녀는 '치즈'라고 말씀하시면서 나의 사진을 찍으셨어. |
| **convenient**<br>[kənvíːnjənt]<br>a. 편리한 | Bomi, it's really convenient to take pictures with my cell phone.<br>보미, 내 휴대 전화로 사진 찍는 것이 정말 편리하구나.<br>• convenience  n. 편리함 |

### culture
[kʌ́ltʃər]
n. 문명, 문화

It's wonderful that you enjoy modern culture.
현대 문명을 즐기시니 정말 멋져요.
- cultural  a. 문화의

### rent
[rént]
v. 대여하다  n. 집세, 임대료

I want to rent a computer.
나는 컴퓨터를 대여하고 싶어.
- rent - rented - rented

### member
[mémbər]
n. 회원, 일원

I can't send messages to my community members.
나는 동호회 회원들에게 메시지를 보낼 수가 없어.

### matter
[mǽtər]
n. 문제, 중요성
v. 문제가 되다, 중요하다

Grandma, what's the matter with your computer?
할머니, 컴퓨터에 무슨 문제가 있나요?

### repair
[ri:péər]
n. 수리, 수선
v. 수리하다

I called a repair person because it's broken.
그것이 고장이 나서 정비사를 불렀어.
- repairable  a. 수리 가능한

### library
[láibrèri]
n. 도서관

You can use a computer at the library.
도서관에서 컴퓨터 사용하실 수 있으세요.

### sociable
[sóuʃəbəl]
a. 사교성 있는

By the way, grandma, you're becoming more sociable.
그런데 할머니, 점점 더 사교적으로 변하시네요.
- society  n. 사회, 사교  - social  a. 사회적인

## belong
[bilɔ́ːŋ]
v. ~에 속하다, 소속하다

Do you belong to the Internet fishing community?
인터넷 낚시 동호회 소속이세요?
- belonging  n. 소유물  • belong to  ~에 속하다
- belong - belonged - belonged

## join
[dʒɔ́in]
v. 가입하다

Yeah, I joined it last month.
그럼, 지난달에 가입했어.
- join - joined - joined

## last
[lǽːst]
a. 지난, 마지막의

Yeah, I joined it last month.
그럼, 지난달에 가입했어.

## fishing
[fíʃiŋ]
n. 낚시

You know, grandpa and I like fishing.
너도 알다시피 할아버지와 나는 낚시를 좋아해.
- fish  v. 낚시하다

## information
[ìnfərméiʃən]
n. 정보

Do you get a lot of information about fishing?
낚시에 관한 정보도 많이 얻나요?
- inform  v. 정보를 제공하다

## island
[áilənd]
n. 섬

Sure. Grandpa and I are going to go fishing on an island next month with the members.
물론이지. 할아버지와 나는 회원들하고 다음 달에 섬으로 낚시를 갈 거야.

## full
[fúl]
a. 가득 찬

You two are full of energy.
두 분은 정말 에너지가 넘치세요.
- be full of  ~로 가득차다

# Check Again!

**A** Translate each word or expression into Korean.

1. last ........................
2. information ........................
3. library ........................
4. sociable ........................
5. technology ........................
6. modern ........................
7. graduation ........................
8. ceremony ........................
9. rent ........................
10. culture ........................

**B** Translate each word or expression into English.

1. 사진을 찍다 ........................
2. 가입하다 ........................
3. 회원 ........................
4. 수리하다 ........................
5. 문제, 중요성 ........................

**C** Fill in the blank with the appropriate word. Refer to the Korean.

1. Jenny tried to c_____ me up.
   제니는 나를 기분 좋게 하려고 애를 썼다.

2. What's the m_____ with your MP3 player?
   네 MP3 플레이어에 무슨 문제가 있니?

3. We b_____ to the surfing community. Would you like to join us?
   우리는 서핑 동호회에 가입되어 있어. 너도 가입할래?

4. The cupboard is f_____ of instant noodles.
   그 찬장은 인스턴트 국수로 가득 차 있다.

5. It is c_____ to ride the subway during rush hour.
   러시 아워에는 지하철을 타는 것이 편리하다.

# Household appliances

1. blender 블렌더
2. toaster 토스터
3. microwave 전자레인지
4. vacuum cleaner 청소기
5. washing machine 세탁기
6. iron 다리미
7. laptop 노트북 컴퓨터
8. coffee machine 커피 머신
9. refrigerator 냉장고
10. cassette tape recorder 카세트 테이프 레코더

- You can make fruit juice **with a blender**.
  당신은 블렌더로 과일 주스를 만들 수 있어요.

- You can make toast **with a toaster**.
  당신은 토스터로 토스트를 만들 수 있어요.

- You can have your clothes pressed **with an iron**.
  당신은 다리미로 옷을 다릴 수 있어요.

- You can clean the floor **with a vacuum cleaner**.
  당신은 진공 청소기로 바닥을 청소할 수 있어요.

- You can play computer games **with a laptop**.
  당신은 노트북으로 컴퓨터 게임을 할 수 있어요.

- You can wash your clothes **with a washing machine**.
  당신은 세탁기로 빨래를 할 수 있어요.

- You can listen to music **with a cassette tape recorder**.
  당신은 카세트 테이프 레코더로 음악을 들을 수 있어요.

*Culture Plus*

**In a lab** 실험실에서
- alcohol lamp 알코올램프
- test tube 시험관
- thermometer 온도계
- solution 용액
- measuring flask 플라스크
- filter paper 거름종이
- material 물질, 재료

- solid 고체
- liquid 액체
- gas 기체

Chapter 11. Technology **225**

# STORYTELLING VOCABULARY
## GREEN

## Chapter 12. Nature and Space

**Unit 30.** We need to reduce garbage.

**Unit 31.** We're thinking of going on a balloon ride.

**Unit 32.** We had a good time.

# Chapter 12
# Nature and Space

## Unit 30. We need to reduce garbage.

talk about **pollution**

**use** old jeans **and make** a wallet

**make** soap **out of** used oil

**sprout** from the bottles

# Episode

Bomi: We **discussed** an interesting **topic** in class. • We talked about **pollution**.

Sara: That's a huge **global** issue these days.

Bomi: The **environment** is so important. • It **affects** us all the time. • And it **treats** us all the same. • We are all **equally** affected. • One thing everyone can do is to **reduce** the amount of garbage we produce.

Sara: Yes, we can **reuse** things. • Take a look at my new **wallet**. • I used my old **jeans** to make it.

Bomi: Were they out of **fashion**?

Sara: Yes, but now they are still being **useful** as a wallet!

Bomi: My mom makes our **soap**. • She makes it out of used **cooking oil**!

Sara: My mom reuses **empty** plastic bottles. • She **grows** plants in them. • I sometimes help her put in the flower **seeds**. • Soon flowers will **sprout** from the **bottles**!

---

보미: 우리는 수업시간에 재미있는 주제를 토론했어. 오염에 대해 이야기했어.

사라: 그건 요새 중요한 세계적 문제야.

보미: 환경은 아주 중요한 거잖아. 늘 우리에게 영향을 미치는 거니까. 그리고 환경은 우리 모두를 똑같이 취급해. 우리 모두 똑같게 영향을 받아. 모든 사람이 할 수 있는 건 우리가 배출하는 쓰레기의 양을 줄이는 거야.

사라: 그래, 우리는 물건을 재사용할 수 있어. 내 새로운 지갑을 좀 봐. 나는 옛날 청바지를 사용해서 그걸 만들었어.

보미: 청바지가 유행이 지난 거였니?

사라: 응, 하지만 이제는 지갑으로 여전히 유용해!

보미: 우리 엄마는 우리 집 비누를 만드셔. 엄마는 사용한 식용유로 비누를 만드시는 거야.

사라: 우리 엄마는 빈 플라스틱 병을 다시 쓰셔. 그 안에 식물을 키우셔. 나는 가끔 엄마를 도와 꽃씨를 심기도 해. 곧 병에서 꽃들이 나기 시작할 거야.

## discuss
[diskʌ́s]
v. 토론하다, 논의하다

We **discussed** an interesting topic in class.
우리는 수업시간에 재미있는 주제를 토론했어.
- **discussion**  n. 토론, 토의
- discuss - discussed - discussed

## topic
[tápik]
n. 논제, 주제

We discussed an interesting **topic** in class.
우리는 수업시간에 재미있는 주제를 토론했어.

## pollution
[pəlúːʃən]
n. 공해, 오염

We talked about **pollution**.
우리는 오염에 대해 이야기했어.
- **pollute**  v. 오염시키다   • **polluted**  a. 오염된

## global
[glóubəl]
a. 세계적인, 전 세계의

That's a huge **global** issue these days.
그건 요새 중요한 세계적 문제야.
- **globe**  n. 지구

## environment
[inváiərənmənt]
n. 환경

The **environment** is so important.
환경은 아주 중요해.
- **environmental**  a. 환경의, 주위의

## affect
[əfékt]
v. ~에 영향을 미치다
n. 영향

It **affects** us all the time.
늘 우리에게 영향을 미치는 거야.
- affect - affected - affected

## treat
[tríːt]
v. 대우하다, 취급하다

And it **treats** us all the same.
그리고 환경은 우리 모두를 똑같이 취급해.
- treat - treated - treated

## equally
[íːkwəli]
ad. 똑같게, 균등하게

We are all equally affected.
우리 모두 똑같게 영향을 받아.

- equal   a. 같은, 동등한

## reduce
[ridjúːs]
v. 줄이다

One thing everyone can do is to reduce the amount of garbage we produce.
모든 사람이 할 수 있는 건 우리가 배출하는 쓰레기의 양을 줄이는 거야.

- reduction   n. 감소, 하락
- reduce - reduced - reduced

## reuse
[riːjúːz]
v. 다시 사용하다   n. 재사용

Yes, we can reuse things.
그래, 우리는 물건을 재사용할 수 있어.

- use   v. 사용하다
- reusable   a. 재사용할 수 있는   • reused   a. 재생한
- reuse - reused - reused

## wallet
[wάlit]
n. 지갑

Take a look at my new wallet.
내 새로운 지갑을 좀 봐.

## jeans
[dʒíːnz]
n. 청바지

I used my old jeans to make it.
나는 옛날 청바지를 사용해서 그걸 만들었어.

## fashion
[fǽʃən]
n. 유행, 패션

Were they out of fashion?
유행이 지난 거였니?

- out of fashion   유행이 지난
- in fashion   유행하고 있는

Chapter 12. Nature and Space

## useful
[jú:sfəl]
a. 유용한

Yes, but now they are still being useful as a wallet!
응, 하지만 이제는 지갑으로 여전히 유용해!

- useless  a. 쓸모없는, 무익한

## soap
[sóup]
n. 비누

My mom makes our soap.
우리 엄마는 우리 집 비누를 만드셔.

## cooking oil
[kúkiŋ ɔil]
식용유

She makes it out of used cooking oil!
사용한 식용유로 비누를 만드시는 거야.

## empty
[émpti]
a. 텅 빈

My mom reuses empty plastic bottles.
우리 엄마는 빈 플라스틱 병을 다시 쓰셔.

## grow
[gróu]
v. 기르다, 재배하다

She grows plants in them.
그 안에 식물을 키우셔.

- growth  n. 성장, 재배, 배양
- grow - grew - grown

## seed
[síːd]
n. 씨앗  v. 씨를 뿌리다

I sometimes help her put in the flower seeds.
나는 가끔 그녀를 도와 꽃씨를 심기도 해.

## sprout
[spráut]
v. 싹트다, 나기 시작하다  n. 싹

Soon flowers will sprout from the bottles!
곧 병에서 꽃들이 나기 시작할 거야.

- sprout - sprouted - sprouted

## bottle
[bátl]
n. 병

Soon flowers will sprout from the bottles!
곧 병에서 꽃들이 나기 시작할 거야.

# Check Again!

**A** Translate each word or expression into Korean.

1. pollution ..................................
2. global ..................................
3. environment ..................................
4. discuss ..................................
5. equally ..................................
6. reduce ..................................
7. useful ..................................
8. empty ..................................
9. seed ..................................
10. sprout ..................................

**B** Translate each word or expression into English.

1. 논제, 주제 ..................................
2. ~에 영향을 미치다 ..................................
3. 다시 사용하다 ..................................
4. 지갑 ..................................
5. 기르다 ..................................

**C** Fill in the blank with the appropriate word. Refer to the Korean.

1. The faded j_____ Helen wore today looked really cool.
   헬렌이 오늘 입은 색바랜 청바지는 아주 멋져 보였어요.

2. I love the smell of this strawberry-scented s_____.
   나는 이 딸기향 비누의 냄새가 너무 좋아요.

3. Baggy pants are coming back into f_____.
   헐렁한 바지가 다시 유행하기 시작해요.

4. Some people use less c_____ oil by using a sprayer.
   어떤 사람들은 분무기를 이용해서 식용유를 덜 사용해요.

5. She wants everyone to t_____ her like a princess.
   그녀는 모든 사람이 자신을 공주처럼 대해주기를 원해요.

Chapter 12. Nature and Space  **233**

# Chapter 12
# Nature and Space

## Unit 31. We're thinking of going on a balloon ride.

**look at** an interesting **article**

**go on a** balloon **ride**

**pilot** the balloon

**land safely** on the ground

# Episode

Dear Diary,

Dad and I are looking at an interesting **article** in the **papers**. • It's about **leisure activities**. • There will be a **hot-air balloon** festival tomorrow. • We're thinking of going on a **balloon ride**. • We can enjoy the beautiful **scenery** all around. • It will be good for the **mind** and body.

The article says there is a **balloonist**. • He **pilots** the balloon. • It's **filled** with gas. • The balloonist sometimes lets you help **inflate** the balloon! • After the balloon starts its flight, the balloonist **controls** it and follows a set **course**. • About an hour later, he will **land** it safely on the ground. • Hot-air balloons are usually safe from **accidents**. • And tomorrow's weather **forecast** is very good. • It says the **wind** will be **mild**. • What does this **mean**? • **Perfect** weather for a balloon ride!

---

다이어리에게,
아빠와 나는 신문에서 재미있는 기사를 살펴보고 있어. 그것은 여가 활동에 관한 거야. 내일 열기구 축제가 있을 거래. 우리는 열기구를 탈까 생각 중이야. 사방의 아름다운 풍경을 감상할 수 있어. 몸과 마음에 도움이 될 거야.
기사에 의하면 열기구 비행사가 있대. 그는 열기구를 조정해. 열기구는 가스로 채워져. 가끔 비행사가 열기구를 부풀리는 일을 도와주게 해준대! 열기구가 비행을 시작한 후 열기구 비행사가 그것을 통제하고 정해진 경로를 따라가. 한 시간쯤 후에 그는 안전하게 땅 위로 열기구를 착륙시킬 거야. 보통 열기구는 사고부터 안전해. 게다가 내일 일기예보가 아주 좋아. 내일 바람이 약할 거래. 이것은 무슨 의미일까? 열기구 타기에 딱 좋은 날씨라는 거야!

## article
[ɑ́ːrtikl]
n. 기사, 논설

Dad and I are looking at an interesting article in the papers.
아빠와 나는 신문에서 재미있는 기사를 살펴보고 있어.

## paper
[péipər]
n. 신문, 종이

Dad and I are looking at an interesting article in the papers.
아빠와 나는 신문에서 재미있는 기사를 살펴보고 있어.

## leisure
[líːʒər]
n. 여가, 자유시간

It's about leisure activities.
그것은 여가 활동에 관한 거야.

## activity
[æktívəti]
n. 활동, 운동

It's about leisure activities.
그것은 여가 활동에 관한 거야.

## hot-air balloon
[hɑ́tɛər bəlúːn]
열기구

There will be a hot-air balloon festival tomorrow.
내일 열기구 축제가 있을 거야.

## balloon ride
[bəlúːn ráid]
열기구 타기

We're thinking of going on a balloon ride.
우리는 열기구를 탈까 생각 중이야.

## scenery
[síːnəri]
n. 풍경

We can enjoy the beautiful scenery all around.
사방의 아름다운 풍경을 감상할 수 있어.

## mind
[máind]
n. 마음, 정신

It will be good for the mind and body.
몸과 마음에 도움이 될 거야.

## balloonist
[bəlúːnist]
n. 열기구 비행사

The article says there is a balloonist.
기사에 의하면 열기구 비행사가 있대.

## pilot
[páilət]
v. 조정하다

He pilots the balloon.
그는 열기구를 조정해.

- pilot - piloted - piloted

## fill
[fíl]
v. 채우다

It's filled with gas.
그것은 가스로 채워져.

- be filled with ~으로 채워지다
- fill - filled - filled

## inflate
[infléit]
v. (풍선 등을) 부풀게 하다

The balloonist sometimes lets you help inflate the balloon!
가끔 비행사가 열기구를 부풀리는 일을 도와주게 해준대!

- inflation  n. 팽창, 부풀리기
- inflate - inflated - inflated

## control
[kəntróul]
v. 통제하다

After the balloon starts its flight, the balloonist controls it and follows a set course.
열기구가 비행을 시작한 후 열기구 비행사가 그것을 통제하고 정해진 경로를 따라가.

- control - controlled - controlled

## course
[kɔ́ːrs]
n. 경로, 진로

After the balloon starts its flight, the balloonist controls it and follows a set course.
열기구가 비행을 시작한 후 열기구 비행사가 그것을 통제하고 정해진 경로를 따라가.

## land
[lǽnd]
v. 착륙시키다, 착륙하다
n. 땅, 육지

About an hour later, he will land it safely on the ground.
한 시간쯤 후에 그는 안전하게 땅 위로 열기구를 착륙시킬 거야.
- land - landed - landed

## accident
[ǽksidənt]
n. 사고

Hot-air balloons are usually safe from accidents.
보통 열기구는 사고로부터 안전해.

## forecast
[fɔ́ːrkæst]
n. 예보, 예상  v. 예보하다

And tomorrow's weather forecast is very good.
게다가 내일 일기예보가 아주 좋아.

## wind
[wínd]
n. 바람

It says the wind will be mild.
내일 바람이 약할 거래.
- windy  a. 바람 부는, 심한

## mild
[máild]
a. 온화한, 순한

It says the wind will be mild.
내일 바람이 약할 거래.

## mean
[míːn]
v. 의미하다

What does this mean?
이것은 무슨 의미일까?
- meaning  n. 의미
- mean - meant - meant

## perfect
[pə́ːrfikt]
a. 완벽한  v. 완성하다

Perfect weather for a balloon ride!
열기구 타기에 딱 좋은 날씨라는 거야!
- perfection  n. 완전, 완벽

# Check Again!

**A** Translate each word or expression into Korean.

1. article _____
2. balloon ride _____
3. scenery _____
4. balloonist _____
5. inflate _____
6. activity _____
7. control _____
8. accident _____
9. forecast _____
10. mild _____

**B** Translate each word or expression into English.

1. 마음, 정신 _____
2. 조정하다 _____
3. 경로, 진로 _____
4. 여가, 자유시간 _____
5. 완벽한 _____

**C** Fill in the blank with the appropriate word. Refer to the Korean.

1. The h_____ balloon sailed freely in the clear sky.
   열기구는 맑은 하늘에 자유롭게 날아갔어요.

2. His eyes were f_____ with deep sorrow.
   그의 눈에는 깊은 슬픔이 가득했어요.

3. I can't quite figure out what it all m_____.
   나는 이 모든 일이 무엇을 의미하는지 정확하게 파악할 수가 없어요.

4. The bank is c_____ by a private company.
   그 은행은 한 개인 회사에 의해 통제되고 있습니다.

5. The delayed plane finally l_____ at the airport.
   연착된 비행기가 드디어 공항에 착륙했어요.

# Chapter 12
# Nature and Space

Unit 32. We had a good time.

**be about to** go out

**blow up** a balloon

**make hair stand up** straight

**make the balloon stick** on the wall

# Episode

Dear Diary,

Hoony and I **were about to** go out. ● But **suddenly**, it started to rain. ● We could **hear thunder**, too. ● Hoony wanted to do an **experiment**. ● "I'll be the **leader**," he said. ● First, Hoony **blew** up a balloon. ● "Rub this on your head," he said. ● The balloon made my **hair** stand up **straight**! ● Then Hoony made the balloon **stick** on the wall! ● "What's the **secret**?" I asked. ● "The balloon has **static** electricity," Hoony said. ● "It's okay to **touch** it. ● Static electricity isn't **dangerous**," Hoony **explained**. ● "You can use static electricity to make a lemon **battery**." ● "We just need a lemon and a few **tools**," Hoony said.

It was very **strange**. ● Hoony's brain was very **active** today. ● He was like a real **scientist**.

It's interesting that a lemon can be used as a **medium** to create electricity.

---

다이어리에게,
후니와 나는 막 나가려는 참이었어. 그런데 갑자기 비가 오기 시작했어. 우리는 천둥소리도 들을 수 있었어. 후니는 실험을 하고 싶어했어. "내가 리더를 할래." 그가 말했어. 우선, 후니가 풍선 하나를 불었어. "이것을 머리 위에 문질러봐." 그가 말했어. 풍선이 내 머리카락을 곧게 서도록 만들었어! 그리고 후니는 풍선을 벽에 붙게 했어! "비밀이 뭐야?" 나는 물었어. "풍선에 정전기가 생긴 거야" 그가 말했어. "그것을 만져도 괜찮아. 정전기는 위험하지 않아." 후니가 설명했어. "정전기를 이용해서 레몬 전지를 만들 수 있어." "그냥 레몬과 몇 가지 도구만 있으면 돼"라고 후니가 말했어.
아주 이상했어. 오늘 후니의 두뇌활동이 매우 활발했어. 그는 진짜 과학자 같았어. 레몬이 전기를 일으키는 매체로 사용될 수 있다니 재미있어.

## be about to
[biː əbàut tuː]
지금 막 ~하려고 하다

Hoony and I were about to go out.
후니와 나는 막 나가려는 참이었어.

## suddenly
[sʌ́dnli]
ad. 갑자기

But suddenly, it started to rain.
그런데 갑자기 비가 오기 시작했어.
- sudden  a. 갑작스러운, 뜻밖의

## hear
[híər]
v. 듣다, 들리다

We could hear thunder, too.
우리는 천둥소리도 들을 수 있었어.
- hear - heard - heard

## thunder
[θʌ́ndər]
n. 천둥

We could hear thunder, too.
우리는 천둥소리도 들을 수 있었어.

## experiment
[ikspérəmənt]
n. 실험  v. 실험하다

Hoony wanted to do an experiment.
후니는 실험을 하고 싶어했어.

## leader
[líːdər]
n. 지도자, 리더

"I'll be the leader," he said.
"내가 리더를 할래." 그가 말했어.

## blow
[blóu]
v. 불다

First, Hoony blew up a balloon.
우선, 후니가 풍선 하나를 불었어.
- blow up  부풀리다    • blow - blew - blown

## hair
[hɛər]
n. 머리카락

The balloon made my hair stand up straight!
풍선이 내 머리카락을 곧게 서도록 만들었어!

## straight
[stréit]
a. 곧은, 똑바로 선

The balloon made my hair stand up straight!
풍선이 내 머리카락을 곧게 서도록 만들었어!

## stick
[stík]
v. 붙이다, 찌르다

Then Hoony made the balloon stick on the wall!
그리고 후니는 풍선을 벽에 붙게 했어!

- stick - stuck - stuck

## secret
[síːkrit]
n. 비밀

"What's the secret?" I asked.
"비밀이 뭐야?" 나는 물었어.

## static
[stǽtik]
a. 정적인, 정전기의

"The balloon has static electricity," Hoony said.
"풍선에 정전기가 생긴 거야." 그가 말했어.

## touch
[tʌtʃ]
v. 만지다, 건드리다
n. 만짐, 촉감

"It's okay to touch it. Static electricity isn't dangerous," Hoony explained.
"그것을 만져도 괜찮아. 정전기는 위험하지 않아." 후니가 설명했어.

- touch - touched - touched

## dangerous
[déindʒərəs]
a. 위험한

"It's okay to touch it. Static electricity isn't dangerous," Hoony explained.
"그것을 만져도 괜찮아. 정전기는 위험하지 않아." 후니가 설명했어.

- danger  n. 위험  • dangerously  ad. 위험하게

## explain
[ikspléin]
v. 설명하다

"It's okay to touch it. Static electricity isn't dangerous," Hoony explained.
"그것을 만져도 괜찮아. 정전기는 위험하지 않아." 후니가 설명했어.
- explanation  n. 설명
- explain - explained - explained

## battery
[bǽtəri]
n. 전지, 배터리

You can use static electricity to make a lemon battery.
정전기를 이용해서 레몬 전지를 만들 수 있어.

## tool
[túːl]
n. 도구, 연장

"We just need a lemon and a few tools," Hoony said.
"그냥 레몬과 몇 가지 도구만 있으면 돼"라고 후니가 말했어.

## strange
[stréindʒ]
a. 이상한, 묘한

It was very strange.
아주 이상했어.
- strangely  ad. 이상하게

## active
[ǽktiv]
a. 활동적인, 활발한

Hoony's brain was very active today.
오늘 후니의 두뇌 활동이 매우 활발했어.
- activeness  n. 활발함, 적극성

## scientist
[sáiəntist]
n. 과학자

He was like a real scientist.
그는 진짜 과학자 같았어.
- science  n. 과학  • scientific  a. 과학의, 과학적인

## medium
[míːdiəm]
n. 매체, 매개물

It's interesting that a lemon can be used as a medium to create electricity.
레몬이 전기를 일으키는 매체로 사용될 수 있다니 재미있어.

# Check Again!

**A** Translate each word or expression into Korean.

1. suddenly .................... 2. thunder ....................
3. strange .................... 4. straight ....................
5. secret .................... 6. static ....................
7. medium .................... 8. dangerous ....................
9. battery .................... 10. touch ....................

**B** Translate each word or expression into English.

1. 지도자, 리더 ....................
2. 듣다, 들리다 ....................
3. 붙이다 ....................
4. 도구, 연장 ....................
5. 과학자 ....................

**C** Fill in the blank with the appropriate word. Refer to the Korean.

1. We were just a_____ to have dinner when he came.
   그가 왔을 때 우리는 막 저녁식사를 하려던 참이었어요.

2. We must have b_____ up over a hundred party balloons.
   우리는 파티용 풍선을 아마 100개 이상은 불었을 거예요.

3. He e_____ the process of making paper.
   그는 종이를 만드는 과정을 설명했다.

4. He is the most a_____ and cheerful person I know.
   그는 내가 아는 사람 중 가장 활동적이고 명랑한 사람이에요.

5. They like to do e_____ .
   그들은 실험하는 것을 좋아한다.

Chapter 12. Nature and Space

# Voca Plus!

# The universe

1. comet 혜성
2. sun 태양
3. Mercury 수성
4. Venus 금성
5. Earth 지구
6. Mars 화성
7. Jupiter 목성
8. Saturn 토성
9. Uranus 천왕성
10. Neptune 해왕성

- There are **eight planets** around the sun.
  태양 주위에 8개의 행성이 있어요.

- **Mercury** is the closest to the sun.
  수성은 태양에서 가장 가까와요.

- **Venus** is the second from the sun.
  금성은 태양에서 두 번째로 가까와요.

- **Earth** is the third from the sun.
  지구는 태양에서 세 번째로 가까와요.

- **Mars** is the fourth from the sun.
  화성은 태양에서 네 번째로 가까와요.

- **Jupiter** is the fifth from the sun.
  목성은 태양에서 다섯 번째로 가까와요.

- **Saturn** has rings around it.
  토성에는 둘레에 고리가 있어요.

*Culture Plus*

**Weather** 날씨

+ heavy rain 폭우
+ smog 스모그
+ strong wind 강풍
+ windstorm 회오리 바람
+ tornado 토네이도
+ thunder 천둥
+ lightning 번개

VOCA EDGE_GREEN
# INDEX

## A

| | | | | | |
|---|---|---|---|---|---|
| ability | 88 | ahead | 122 | appoint | 82 |
| able | 88 | air pollution | 187 | appointment | 82 |
| absence | 104 | airport | 82 | appreciate | 172 |
| absent | 104 | aisle | 76 | appreciation | 172 |
| accident | 238 | alcohol lamp | 225 | April Fool | 120 |
| ache | 96 | alike | 138 | April Fool's Day | 165 |
| across | 36 | allow | 178 | Arbor Day | 165 |
| across from | 39 | allowance | 178 | armchair | 39, 106 |
| act | 95 | alone | 62 | armrest | 76 |
| action | 95 | along | 90 | around | 95 |
| active | 244 | ambulance | 122 | arrange | 94 |
| activeness | 244 | America | 77 | arrangement | 94 |
| activity | 236 | American | 77 | arrival | 46 |
| ad | 198 | amuse | 60 | arrive | 46 |
| add | 149 | amused | 60 | art | 55 |
| address | 34 | amusement | 60 | article | 236 |
| advice | 205 | anger | 200 | ATM | 209 |
| advise | 205 | ankle | 115 | attention | 204 |
| aerobics | 99 | announce | 171 | attentive | 204 |
| affect | 230 | announcement | 171 | aunt | 22, 72 |
| afford | 198 | anxiety | 121 | away | 18 |
| affordable | 198 | anxious | 121 | awe | 132 |
| again | 68 | anyway | 206 | awesome | 132 |

| | | apartment | 66 | ## B | |
|---|---|---|---|---|---|
| age | 30 | appear | 83 | bake | 112 |
| aged | 30 | appearance | 83 | bakery | 34, 112 |
| agree | 182 | appendix | 114 | balance | 122 |
| agreeable | 182 | appetite | 112 | balloon ride | 236 |
| agreement | 182 | appetizing | 112 | balloonist | 237 |

| | | |
|---|---|---|
| bandage | 148 | |
| bank book | 209 | |
| bank teller | 209 | |
| baseball diamond | 98 | |
| baseball park | 98 | |
| basic | 95 | |
| basically | 95 | |
| basics | 95 | |
| basketball | 89 | |
| bat | 98 | |
| battery | 244 | |
| be about to | 242 | |
| be oneself | 96 | |
| beautiful | 106, 149 | |
| beauty | 106, 149 | |
| because | 13 | |
| beg | 200 | |
| behind | 39, 99 | |
| belief | 12 | |
| believe | 12 | |
| belong | 222 | |
| belonging | 222 | |
| bench | 61 | |
| bend | 215 | |
| bendable | 215 | |
| between | 39, 183 | |
| big | 143 | |
| bill | 209 | |
| bit | 206 | |
| blanket | 23 | |
| bleed | 148 | |
| blender | 224 | |
| blind | 30 | |
| blond hair | 143 | |
| blood | 148 | |
| blouse | 142 | |
| blow | 154, 242 | |
| boast | 134 | |
| boastful | 134 | |
| body | 115 | |
| boil | 20 | |
| bold | 143 | |
| bone | 156 | |
| bookstore | 35, 38 | |
| boost | 89 | |
| border | 183 | |
| boring | 178 | |
| borrow | 204 | |
| boss | 20 | |
| bottle | 232 | |
| bowling | 99 | |
| brain | 114, 156 | |
| branch | 156 | |
| brand-new | 204 | |
| brave | 133 | |
| bravely | 133 | |
| bravery | 133 | |
| break | 121 | |
| breath | 204 |
| breathe | 204 |
| bright | 120 |
| bring | 121 |
| broadcasting | 132 |
| broom | 164 |
| brother | 22 |
| bubble | 154 |
| bullpen | 98 |
| burn | 139 |
| bus stop | 38 |
| business | 150 |
| by | 39 |

## C

| | |
|---|---|
| calf | 115 |
| candle | 164 |
| candy | 105, 164 |
| capital | 72 |
| care | 29 |
| careless | 29 |
| carelessness | 29 |
| carpet | 29 |
| carry | 214 |
| cash | 209 |
| cashier | 208 |
| cassette tape recorder | 224 |
| catcher | 98 |
| ceiling | 39 |
| celebrate | 94 |

| | | | | | | | |
|---|---|---|---|---|---|---|---|
| celebration | 94 | Christmas | 165 | control | 237 |
| century | 160 | church | 35 | convenience | 220 |
| ceremony | 220 | classmate | 138 | convenience store | 38 |
| chalk | 54 | classroom | 54 | convenient | 220 |
| chalkboard | 54 | clever | 216 | conversation | 162 |
| chance | 18 | clinic | 105 | converse | 162 |
| change | 95 | closet | 39 | cook | 20, 111 |
| changeable | 95 | coast | 172 | cooker | 111 |
| charm | 44 | coastal | 172 | cooking oil | 232 |
| charming | 44 | coffee machine | 224 | cool | 205 |
| chase | 51 | coin | 209 | copy | 126 |
| chat | 192 | collect | 30 | cost | 74 |
| cheap | 193 | collection | 30 | costume party | 164 |
| cheaper | 193 | collective | 30 | couch | 39 |
| cheapest | 193 | color | 177 | count | 154 |
| check | 209 | colorful | 177 | countable | 154 |
| checkup | 127 | Columbus Day | 165 | counter | 208 |
| cheek | 84 | comet | 246 | coupon | 194 |
| cheer | 220 | comic book | 28 | courage | 134 |
| cheerful | 143, 220 | common | 88 | courageous | 134 |
| chest | 115 | communicate | 162 | course | 237 |
| chew | 111 | communication | 162 | cousin | 22, 82 |
| China | 77 | compact | 216 | cover | 186 |
| Chinese | 77 | company | 150 | cradle | 23 |
| choice | 112 | computer | 54 | create | 155 |
| choke | 29 | concert | 198 | creation | 155 |
| choose | 112 | congratulate | 133 | creative | 155 |
| chopsticks | 128 | congratulation | 133 | credit card | 208 |
| chores | 128 | contest | 214 | crosswalk | 38 |

| | | | | | | | |
|---|---|---|---|---|---|---|---|
| crossword puzzle | 54 | delivery | 133 | division | 128 |
| crowd | 83 | dentist | 160 | double | 127 |
| crowded | 83 | department store | 193 | downtown | 214 |
| crush | 12 | depth | 204 | draw | 148 |
| cultural | 221 | desert | 184 | drawer | 30 |
| culture | 221 | desk | 54 | dress shirt | 142 |
| curiosity | 83 | dessert | 73 | drive | 216 |
| curious | 83 | diaper | 23 | driver | 216 |
| curl | 84 | diet | 112 | duck | 52 |
| curly | 84 | difference | 139 | dugout | 98 |
| curly hair | 142 | different | 139 | during | 140 |
| custom | 73 | differently | 139 | Dutch | 77 |
| cut | 148 | difficult | 184 | dye | 178 |
| cute | 204 | difficulty | 184 | dyed | 178 |

## D

| | | | | | |
|---|---|---|---|---|---|
| | | digital camera | 150 | dynamic | 143 |
| dancing | 99 | diligent | 143 | | |

## E

| | | | | | |
|---|---|---|---|---|---|
| danger | 243 | dinner | 171 | earlier | 162 |
| dangerous | 243 | direction | 35 | Earth | 246 |
| dangerously | 243 | disappoint | 46 | education | 184 |
| date | 138 | disappointed | 46 | educational | 184 |
| dated | 138 | disappointment | 46 | effort | 45 |
| daughter | 23 | discuss | 230 | either | 176 |
| daughter-in-law | 23 | discussion | 230 | elbow | 115 |
| deaf | 28 | disease | 105 | electricity | 194 |
| decide | 96 | dish | 68 | elementary | 138 |
| decision | 96 | disposable | 187 | embarrass | 14 |
| deep | 204 | distance | 134 | embarrassed | 14 |
| degree | 73 | distant | 134 | embarrassment | 14 |
| deliver | 133 | divide | 128 | empty | 232 |

| | | | | | |
|---|---|---|---|---|---|
| encourage | 134 | exception | 206 | feather | 172 |
| energetic | 67 | exercise | 126 | feet | 115 |
| energy | 67 | expensive | 198 | festival | 18 |
| engineer | 162 | experiment | 242 | fever | 104 |
| England | 77 | explain | 160, 244 | feverish | 104 |
| English | 55, 77 | explanation | 160, 244 | fill | 237 |
| enough | 184 | explanatory | 160 | filter paper | 225 |
| enter | 121, 199 | express | 178 | final | 84 |
| entrance | 121 | express lane | 208 | finally | 84 |
| envious | 133 | expression | 178 | fire station | 38 |
| environment | 187, 230 | expressive | 178 | firm | 176 |
| environmental | 230 | **F** | | firmly | 176 |
| envy | 133 | face | 115 | first-aid | 148 |
| equal | 231 | factory | 162 | first base | 98 |
| equally | 231 | fail | 96 | fish | 222 |
| eraser | 54 | failure | 96 | fishing | 222 |
| eve | 170 | fair | 176 | fit | 206 |
| even | 139 | fame | 206 | fitness | 206 |
| evenly | 139 | famous | 206 | flag | 88 |
| everywhere | 30 | far | 170 | flat | 154 |
| exact | 134 | farmer | 162 | flight | 52, 161 |
| exactly | 134 | fashion | 231 | flight attendant | 76 |
| exam | 106 | fast food | 110 | flour | 215 |
| examination | 106 | fasten | 62 | flu | 104 |
| examine | 106 | fat | 143 | fly | 52, 161 |
| example | 192 | father | 22 | folk | 66 |
| excellence | 200 | favor | 82 | folklore | 66 |
| excellent | 200 | favorable | 82 | follow | 62 |
| except | 206 | favorite | 132, 205 | follower | 62 |

| | | | | | |
|---|---|---|---|---|---|
| following | 62 | gas station | 38 | hamster | 120 |
| fool | 134 | gate | 156 | handbag | 142 |
| foolish | 134 | gather | 67 | handout | 177 |
| foot | 115 | genius | 216 | handsome | 83 |
| football game | 50 | gentle | 143 | hard | 122 |
| forecast | 238 | German | 77 | hardly | 122 |
| foreign | 67 | Germany | 77 | hardworking | 172 |
| foreigner | 67 | gesture | 183 | harm | 161 |
| forget | 140 | ghost | 164 | harmful | 161 |
| forgetful | 140 | global | 230 | hate | 199 |
| forgettable | 140 | globe | 230 | hatred | 199 |
| forgive | 206 | glove | 98 | head | 115 |
| forgiveness | 206 | glue | 149 | headphones | 76 |
| free | 18, 60 | goalkeeper | 51 | health | 110 |
| freedom | 18 | good-looking | 44 | healthy | 110 |
| freeze | 14 | goods | 193 | hear | 242 |
| freezing | 14 | grade | 46 | heart | 114 |
| fried | 110 | graduate | 220 | heavily | 216 |
| friend | 139 | graduation | 220 | heavy | 216 |
| friendly | 139, 143 | grain | 112 | heavy rain | 247 |
| frozen | 14 | grandparent | 13, 22 | height | 61 |
| fry | 110 | greet | 214 | help | 134 |
| full | 222 | greeting | 214 | hero | 51 |
| furniture | 214 | gross | 149 | heroine | 51 |
| future | 140 | grow | 82, 232 | high | 61 |
| **G** | | growth | 82, 232 | high chair | 23 |
| garage | 128 | guess | 150 | high heels | 142 |
| garbage | 128 | **H** | | historical | 161 |
| gas | 225 | hair | 243 | history | 44, 55, 161 |

| | | | | | |
|---|---|---|---|---|---|
| hobby | 99 | impression | 150 | jeans | 231 |
| hold | 84 | impressive | 150 | job | 200 |
| holiday | 72, 126 | in | 99 | jogging | 99 |
| Holland | 77 | in front of | 19, 39, 99 | join | 222 |
| home plate | 98 | Independence Day | 165 | Jupiter | 246 |
| homeroom teacher | 54 | indoor | 50 | just in time | 36 |
| honest | 134 | indoors | 50 | | |

### K

| | | | | | |
|---|---|---|---|---|---|
| honestly | 134 | inflate | 237 | kindergarten | 38 |
| honesty | 134 | inflation | 237 | knee | 115 |
| horseback riding | 99 | inform | 222 | knit | 95 |
| hospital | 38 | information | 222 | knitting | 95, 99 |
| host | 94 | interest | 74 | knowledge | 184 |
| hot-air balloon | 236 | interesting | 74 | knowledgeable | 184 |
| hot dog | 149 | international | 192 | Korea | 77 |
| huge | 82 | intersection | 38 | Korean | 55, 77 |

### L

| | | | | | |
|---|---|---|---|---|---|
| hunger | 68 | interview | 132 | | |
| hungry | 68 | introduce | 12 | lab | 225 |
| hurt | 104 | introduction | 12 | land | 238 |
| hurtful | 104 | invent | 162 | language | 183 |
| husband | 23 | invention | 162 | laptop | 224 |

### I

| | | | | | |
|---|---|---|---|---|---|
| | | inventor | 162 | large intestine | 114 |
| idea | 51 | invitation | 13, 216 | last | 222 |
| ideal | 51 | invite | 13, 216 | leader | 242 |
| imaginary | 160, 182 | iron | 224 | leave | 205 |
| imagination | 160, 182 | island | 222 | leg | 115 |

### J

| | | | | | |
|---|---|---|---|---|---|
| imaginative | 160 | | | leisure | 236 |
| imagine | 160, 182 | jack-o-lantern | 164 | lend | 204 |
| impatient | 96 | Japan | 77 | lesson | 18 |
| impress | 150 | Japanese | 77 | liar | 120 |

| | | | | | |
|---|---|---|---|---|---|
| library | 221 | marriage | 13 | midnight | 72 |
| lie | 30, 120 | marry | 13 | mild | 238 |
| light | 39, 194 | Mars | 246 | milk bottle | 23 |
| lightning | 247 | mask | 67, 164 | million | 90 |
| like | 127 | mass-produce | 161 | mind | 236 |
| line | 60, 182 | mass-produced | 161 | mirror | 105 |
| liquid | 225 | match | 52 | miss | 34, 62 |
| listen | 19 | material | 225 | missing | 62 |
| literature | 55 | math | 55 | mistake | 62 |
| liver | 114 | matter | 94, 221 | mistaken | 62 |
| location | 34 | meal | 172 | mitt | 98 |
| look | 12 | mean | 238 | mix | 215 |
| loose | 176 | meaning | 238 | mixture | 215 |
| loosen | 176 | measuring flask | 225 | mobile | 23 |
| lose | 14 | measuring tape | 54 | model | 198 |
| loss | 14 | meat | 110 | modern | 220 |
| luck | 46 | medical | 106 | money | 192 |
| luckily | 36 | medicine | 106 | monster | 105 |
| lucky | 46 | medium | 244 | mother | 22 |
| lungs | 114 | member | 221 | mountain climbing | 99 |

## M

| | | | | | |
|---|---|---|---|---|---|
| | | Memorial Day | 165 | mouse | 120 |
| machine | 215 | memorize | 45 | move | 51 |
| magazine | 111 | memory | 45 | movement | 51 |
| magic | 60 | Mercury | 246 | mumps | 106 |
| main | 73 | mess | 30 | muscles | 143 |
| mainly | 73 | message | 182 | museum | 66 |
| manager | 127 | messy | 30 | music | 55 |
| map | 184 | microwave | 224 | | |
| market | 193 | middle | 178 | nation | 88 |

## N

| | | | | | | | |
|---|---|---|---|---|---|---|---|
| national | 88 | occur | 160 | pattern | 149 |
| nationality | 77 | occurrence | 160 | PE | 50 |
| natural | 138 | ocean | 68 | peace | 183 |
| naturally | 138 | often | 216 | peaceful | 183 |
| nature | 138 | oil spill | 171, 187 | perfect | 238 |
| near | 90, 99 | on the corner of | 39 | perfection | 238 |
| nearly | 90 | outdoor | 193 | person | 133 |
| neck | 115 | outgoing | 139, 143 | personal | 133 |
| need | 112 | outside | 50 | personality | 143, 178 |
| needful | 112 | overhead compartment | 76 | phone call | 72 |
| needy | 112 | overpass | 38 | photo | 132 |

## P

| | | | | | | | |
|---|---|---|---|---|---|---|---|
| neighbor | 171 | | | photograph | 199 |
| neighborhood | 171 | pack | 73 | photographer | 132 |
| neighboring | 171 | package | 73 | physical education | 55 |
| neither | 72 | pain | 160 | pick | 82, 186 |
| nephew | 23 | painful | 160 | picture | 39, 220 |
| Neptune | 246 | pair | 172 | piece | 29 |
| nervous | 13 | paper | 54, 236 | pilot | 161, 237 |
| nervously | 13 | parade | 62 | pirate | 164 |
| New Year's Day | 165 | parcel | 208 | pitcher | 98 |
| next to | 35, 39 | pardon | 170 | plain | 148 |
| niece | 23 | Parents' Day | 165 | planet | 247 |
| night | 192 | party | 14 | plant | 128 |
| noise | 28 | pass | 36, 60 | plastic bag | 187 |
| noisy | 28 | passenger | 76 | please | 128 |

## O

| | | | | | | | |
|---|---|---|---|---|---|---|---|
| | | past | 160 | pleased | 128 |
| obedience | 19 | path | 90 | pleasure | 128 |
| obedient | 19 | patience | 96 | plentiful | 214 |
| obey | 19 | patient | 96 | plenty | 214 |

| | | | | | | | |
|---|---|---|---|---|---|---|---|
| plug | 194 | | protection | 183 | | refrigerate | 110 |
| polite | 19 | | protective | 183 | | refrigerator | 110, 224 |
| pollute | 230 | | proud | 46 | | regular | 161 |
| polluted | 230 | | pull | 29 | | regulate | 177 |
| pollution | 187, 230 | | pumpkin | 164 | | regulation | 177 |
| popular | 44 | | pupil | 50 | | relative | 68 |
| popularity | 44 | | purple | 178 | | relax | 28 |
| pose | 199 | | | | | relaxation | 28 |

## Q

| | | | | | | | |
|---|---|---|---|---|---|---|---|
| post | 150 | | quick | 36 | | remember | 95, 138 |
| potato | 111 | | quickly | 36 | | remembrance | 95, 138 |
| pour | 121 | | quit | 127 | | rent | 221 |

## R

| | | | | | | | |
|---|---|---|---|---|---|---|---|
| power | 90 | | | | | repair | 221 |
| powerful | 90 | | reach | 171 | | repairable | 221 |
| practice | 154 | | reachable | 171 | | repeat | 89 |
| praise | 45 | | ready | 60 | | repeatedly | 89 |
| praiseworthy | 45 | | really | 172 | | repetition | 89 |
| preparation | 46 | | reason | 177 | | repetitive | 89 |
| prepare | 46 | | reasonable | 177 | | report | 132 |
| present | 94 | | receipt | 208 | | reporter | 132 |
| pride | 46 | | recipe | 20 | | require | 89 |
| princess | 165 | | recover | 106 | | requirement | 89 |
| principal | 54 | | recovery | 106 | | resolute | 126 |
| print | 19 | | recycling | 187 | | resolution | 126 |
| prize | 199 | | recycling bin | 187 | | respect | 88 |
| professional | 156 | | reduce | 231 | | respectable | 88 |
| program | 140 | | reduction | 231 | | respectful | 88 |
| pronounce | 88 | | reflect | 105 | | rest | 90 |
| pronunciation | 88 | | reflection | 105 | | restaurant | 38 |
| protect | 183 | | reflective | 105 | | return | 205 |

| | | | | | | | |
|---|---|---|---|---|---|---|---|
| reusable | 231 | save | 192 | sensory | 139 |
| reuse | 231 | saving | 192 | serve | 215 |
| reused | 231 | scare | 52 | service | 215 |
| review | 45 | scared | 52 | shadow | 155 |
| reviewal | 45 | scarf | 28 | shake | 13 |
| reviewer | 45 | scary | 52 | shame | 52 |
| reward | 200 | scenery | 236 | shameful | 52 |
| rewardless | 200 | schedule | 155 | shape | 154 |
| ride | 60, 90 | school | 38 | sharp | 155 |
| right | 74 | science | 55, 244 | sheet | 215 |
| rinse | 171 | scientific | 244 | shoes | 14 |
| roller skating | 99 | scientist | 244 | shopper | 208 |
| roof | 67 | score | 52 | shopping | 193 |
| rot | 156 | scream | 62 | shopping cart | 208 |
| rotten | 156 | screen | 155 | shopping list | 208 |
| round | 154 | scuba diving | 99 | shoulder | 115 |
| rub | 121 | seafood | 170 | shoulder bag | 142 |
| rude | 18 | seat belt | 76 | shout | 120 |
| rudely | 18 | second base | 98 | show | 88 |
| rug | 39 | secret | 243 | shower | 170 |
| rule | 177 | seed | 232 | shy | 143 |
| ruler | 54 | seem | 74 | sidewalk | 89 |
| run | 120 | seeming | 74 | sightsee | 67 |
| **S** | | seemly | 74 | sightseeing | 67 |
| safe | 61 | selfish | 143 | sign | 83, 126 |
| safely | 61 | send | 150 | signature | 126 |
| safety | 61 | sense | 139 | similar | 89, 140 |
| sale | 194 | sensible | 139 | similarity | 89, 140 |
| Saturn | 246 | sensitive | 139 | similarly | 89, 140 |

| | | |
|---|---|---|
| simple | 148 | |
| simplify | 148 | |
| single | 126 | |
| sister | 22 | |
| skateboard | 198 | |
| skating | 99 | |
| skiing | 99 | |
| skin | 111 | |
| skinny | 111 | |
| skirt | 142, 176 | |
| slice | 127 | |
| slim | 12, 143 | |
| slip | 121, 122 | |
| slippery | 121 | |
| small intestine | 114 | |
| smart | 20 | |
| smell | 20 | |
| smile | 215 | |
| smiling | 215 | |
| smog | 247 | |
| smoke | 127 | |
| sneakers | 142 | |
| soap | 232 | |
| sociable | 221 | |
| social | 221 | |
| social studies | 55 | |
| society | 221 | |
| socks | 95 | |
| soft | 112 | |
| softness | 112 | |
| soldier | 182 | |
| solid | 225 | |
| solution | 225 | |
| someday | 74 | |
| sometimes | 140 | |
| son | 23 | |
| son-in-law | 23 | |
| sore | 104 | |
| soreness | 104 | |
| sound | 104 | |
| spaceship | 140 | |
| spare | 140 | |
| special | 28 | |
| specialize | 28 | |
| spend | 198 | |
| spice | 68 | |
| spicy | 68 | |
| spill | 29 | |
| spoon | 74 | |
| spray | 176 | |
| spread | 139 | |
| sprout | 232 | |
| stand | 199 | |
| starvation | 110 | |
| starve | 110 | |
| starving | 110 | |
| static | 243 | |
| steal | 205 | |
| steward | 76 | |
| stewardess | 76 | |
| stick | 243 | |
| stolen | 205 | |
| stomach | 114 | |
| stop | 122 | |
| story | 66 | |
| straight | 243 | |
| straight hair | 142 | |
| strange | 61, 244 | |
| strangely | 61, 244 | |
| stranger | 61 | |
| strict | 50 | |
| strictly | 50 | |
| stroller | 23 | |
| strong wind | 247 | |
| student | 156 | |
| style | 132 | |
| stylish | 132 | |
| subject | 44, 55 | |
| subway station | 34 | |
| succeed | 200 | |
| success | 200 | |
| sudden | 242 | |
| suddenly | 242 | |
| suit | 96, 142 | |
| suitable | 96 | |
| sun | 246 | |
| sunglasses | 199 | |

| | | |
|---|---|---|
| sunny | 50 | |
| supermarket | 35, 38 | |
| suppose | 138 | |
| surprise | 19 | |
| surprised | 19 | |
| surprising | 19 | |
| swallow | 111 | |
| sweat | 51 | |
| sweaty | 51 | |
| swimming | 99 | |
| swing | 23 | |

## T

| | |
|---|---|
| take | 29 |
| talkative | 143 |
| tall | 143 |
| taste | 68 |
| tasty | 68 |
| teach | 18 |
| teacher | 44 |
| team | 171 |
| technology | 220 |
| test | 45 |
| test tube | 225 |
| textbook | 45, 54 |
| Thanksgiving Day | 165 |
| thermometer | 225 |
| thief | 205 |
| thigh | 115 |
| thin | 14 |
| thing | 214 |
| third base | 98 |
| thirst | 200 |
| thirsty | 200 |
| throat | 114 |
| throw | 186 |
| thunder | 242, 247 |
| ticket | 198 |
| tie | 142 |
| tight | 206 |
| tighten | 206 |
| time | 89 |
| timid | 143 |
| toaster | 224 |
| together | 94 |
| tool | 244 |
| topic | 230 |
| tornado | 247 |
| touch | 243 |
| tour | 73 |
| tourist | 73 |
| towards | 84, 99 |
| toy gun | 28 |
| tradition | 66 |
| traditional | 66 |
| traditionally | 66 |
| trash | 186 |
| travel | 74 |
| tray | 20, 76 |
| treat | 230 |
| treats | 164 |
| trick | 122 |
| trick or treat | 164 |
| trip | 66 |
| T-shirt | 142 |
| turn | 19, 35, 61, 194 |

## U

| | |
|---|---|
| umpire | 98 |
| uncle | 22 |
| underline | 177 |
| unfair | 176 |
| uniform | 177 |
| unique | 67 |
| uniquely | 67 |
| uniqueness | 67 |
| unplug | 194 |
| Uranus | 246 |
| use | 231 |
| useful | 232 |
| useless | 232 |
| U-turn | 36 |

## V

| | |
|---|---|
| vacuum cleaner | 224 |
| vegetable | 110 |
| Venus | 246 |
| village | 170 |
| villager | 170 |
| voice | 104 |

| | |
|---|---|
| voice actor | 155 |
| volunteer | 170 |

## W

| | |
|---|---|
| waist | 115 |
| walk | 186 |
| walker | 23 |
| wallet | 231 |
| war | 182 |
| warm | 94 |
| warm-hearted | 204 |
| warmth | 94 |
| washing machine | 224 |
| waste | 61 |
| wasteful | 61 |
| water pollution | 187 |
| way | 88 |
| weapon | 183 |
| weaponize | 183 |
| wear | 14 |
| weather | 247 |
| wedding | 12 |
| welcome | 84 |
| whole | 112 |
| wife | 23 |
| wind | 238 |
| window | 39, 76 |
| windstorm | 247 |
| windsurfing | 99 |
| windy | 238 |
| wire | 192 |
| wireless | 192 |
| wisdom | 194 |
| wise | 194 |
| witch | 164 |
| without | 34 |
| witty | 143 |
| wonder | 83 |
| wonderful | 83 |
| worse | 111 |
| worst | 111 |
| wrap | 133 |
| wrist | 115 |

## X

| | |
|---|---|
| xylophone | 54 |

## Y

| | |
|---|---|
| yachting | 99 |

VOCA EDGE_GREEN

# Answer Key

## Chapter 1_ Unit 1

### Check Again!

**A**
1. 결혼식
2. 믿다
3. ~처럼 보이다
4. 날씬한, 가는
5. 소개하다, 만나게 해주다
6. 조부모
7. ~때문에
8. 떨다, 흔들다
9. 얻다
10. 창피한, 무안한

**B**
1. thin
2. invite
3. nervous
4. wear
5. have a party

**C**
1. marry
2. crush
3. lost
4. introduce
5. embarrassed

## Chapter 1_ Unit 2

### Check Again!

**A**
1. 축제
2. 자유로운
3. 조리법, 요리법
4. 공손한, 예의바른
5. 쟁반
6. 출력하다
7. ~을 듣다
8. 요리하다
9. ~의 앞에(서)
10. 두목, 대장

**B**
1. chance
2. rude
3. smart
4. surprise
5. boil

**C**
1. away
2. smell
3. teach
4. turned
5. obeys

## Chapter 2_ Unit 3

### Check Again!

**A**
1. 쉬다
2. 어디에나, 도처에
3. 만화책
4. 목도리
5. 잡아당기다
6. 숨막히게 하다
7. 부주의한, 조심성 없는
8. 조각
9. 모으다
10. 지저분한

**B**
1. special
2. blind
3. drawer
4. lie
5. deaf

**C**
1. apart
2. noises
3. spilled(spilt)
4. lying
5. age

## Chapter 2_ Unit 4

### Check Again!

**A**
1. 다행히도
2. 주소, 연설
3. 위치
4. 방향
5. 교회
6. ~의 옆에
7. 지나가다, 통과하다
8. ~의 맞은편에
9. 지하철역
10. 때맞추어

**B**
1. across
2. quickly
3. bookstore
4. pass by
5. ask for directions

**C**
1. supermarket
2. without
3. directions
4. turn
5. missed

## Chapter 3_ Unit 5

### Check Again!

**A**
1. 역사
2. 칭찬하다
3. 테스트
4. 잘생긴
5. 매력적인
6. 행운의
7. 실망시키다
8. 외우다
9. 인기 있는
10. 복습하다

**B**
1. subject
2. textbook
3. arrive
4. grade
5. teacher

**C**
1. proud
2. memorizing
3. effort
4. popular
5. prepare

## Chapter 3_ Unit 6

### Check Again!

**A**
1. 체육
2. 밖에, 바깥에
3. 머리를 홱 숙이다
4. 학생, 제자
5. 움직이다
6. 땀이 나는
7. 생각
8. 뒤쫓다
9. 축구 경기
10. 득점하다, 점수

**B**
1. sunny
2. indoor
3. goalkeeper
4. fly
5. scared

**C**
1. strict
2. move
3. match
4. heroine
5. shame

## Chapter 4_ Unit 7

### Check Again!

**A**
1. 차례, 돌다
2. 즐거움, 재미
3. 낯선 사람
4. 이용권, 지나가다
5. 실수
6. 소리지르다
7. 낭비, 낭비하다
8. 안전
9. 놀이기구, 타다
10. 마법, 마술

**B**
1. ready
2. parade
3. free
4. follow
5. alone

**C**
1. Fasten
2. line
3. missing
4. scream
5. height

## Chapter 4_ Unit 8

### Check Again!

**A**
1. 박물관
2. 지붕
3. 배고픈
4. 관광
5. 다시, 한 번 더
6. 에너지, 힘
7. 민속의
8. 바다
9. 전통의
10. 친척

**B**
1. gather
2. dish
3. tasty
4. foreigner
5. mask

**C**
1. trip
2. spicy
3. story
4. sightseeing
5. unique

# Chapter 4_ Unit 9

## Check Again!

**A**
1. 여행하다
2. 후식
3. 풍습, 관습
4. ~인 듯하다
5. 흥미있는, 재미있는
6. 한밤중, 자정
7. 비용이 들다
8. 온도
9. 오른쪽의
10. 전화를 걺, 통화

**B**
1. main
2. someday
3. aunt
4. tourist
5. holiday

**C**
1. package
2. capital
3. dessert
4. Someday
5. neither

# Chapter 5_ Unit 10

## Check Again!

**A**
1. 환영하다
2. 잘생긴
3. 부탁, 호의
4. 커다란
5. 마중 나가다
6. 약속, 예약
7. 성장하다, 자라다
8. 혼잡한
9. ~을 향하여
10. 들다, 쥐다

**B**
1. cousin
2. sign
3. airport
4. wonder
5. curious

**C**
1. cheek
2. finally
3. curly
4. favor
5. Appearance

# Chapter 5_ Unit 11

## Check Again!

**A**
1. 백만
2. 존경, 존중
3. 요구하다
4. ~을 따라서
5. 타다
6. 강한
7. 비슷한, 유사한
8. 보여주다, 나타내다
9. 길, 도로
10. ~번, ~배

**B**
1. common
2. repeatedly
3. rest
4. national
5. pronounce

**C**
1. boost
2. basketball
3. able
4. sidewalk
5. nearly

# Chapter 5_ Unit 12

## Check Again!

**A**
1. 기초의, 근본의
2. 함께, 같이
3. 문제
4. 행동하다
5. 선물
6. 자연스럽게 행동하다
7. 따뜻한
8. 준비하다
9. 아프다
10. 참을성 있는

**B**
1. change
2. around
3. knitting
4. host
5. decide

**C**
1. remember
2. failed
3. suit
4. celebrate
5. patient

# Chapter 6_ Unit 13

## Check Again!

**A**
1. 안락의자
2. 결석한
3. 질병
4. 진찰하다
5. 거울
6. 독감
7. ~하게 들리다, 소리
8. 반영, 반사
9. 아름다움, 미인
10. 목소리, 음성

**B**
1. hurt
2. recover
3. fever
4. clinic
5. monster

**C**
1. absent
2. reflection
3. exam
4. medicine
5. sore

# Chapter 6_ Unit 14

## Check Again!

**A**
1. 식욕을 돋우는
2. 식이요법
3. 배고픈
4. 피부
5. 고기
6. 냉장고
7. 더 나쁜
8. 부드러운
9. 씹다
10. 선택(권)

**B**
1. need
2. cooker
3. swallow
4. healthy
5. whole

**C**
1. choice
2. bakery
3. starving
4. magazines
5. vegetable

# Chapter 7_ Unit 15

## Check Again!

**A**
1. 외치다
2. 거짓말하다
3. 장난, 속임수
4. 가져오다
5. 붓다
6. 문지르다
7. 미끄러운
8. 들어오다
9. 근심하는
10. 균형

**B**
1. April Fool
2. run out
3. break
4. ambulance
5. hardly

**C**
1. rubbed
2. slipped
3. stop
4. ahead
5. brought

# Chapter 7_ Unit 16

## Check Again!

**A**
1. 휴일, 휴가
2. 차고
3. 결심, 결의
4. 서명하다
5. 식물
6. 담배를 피우다
7. 그만두다, 끊다
8. 매니저, 관리자
9. 가사, 자질구레한 일
10. 쓰레기

**B**
1. copy
2. double
3. checkup
4. divide
5. like

**C**
1. slice
2. single
3. exercise
4. chores
5. pleased

Answer Key 267

## Chapter 7_ Unit 17

### Check Again!

**A**
1. 자랑하다
2. 포장하다
3. 맵시 있는, 멋진
4. 인터뷰하다
5. 부러워하다, 질투하다
6. 전하다, 배달하다
7. 좋아하는
8. 어리석은
9. 멋진, 굉장한
10. 솔직히

**B**
1. congratulation
2. distance
3. broadcasting
4. brave
5. exactly

**C**
1. courage
2. person
3. reporter
4. distance
5. envy

## Chapter 8_ Unit 19

### Check Again!

**A**
1. 베다, 상처를 내다
2. 피
3. 응급 치료의
4. 단순한, 간단한
5. 불쾌한, 구역질 나는
6. 아름다운
7. 게시하다, 정보를 알리다
8. 회사
9. 깊은 인상을 주다
10. 무늬

**B**
1. bandage
2. draw
3. send
4. add
5. glue

**C**
1. digital
2. guess
3. business
4. impressed
5. plain

## Chapter 7_ Unit 18

### Check Again!

**A**
1. 가정하다, 만약 ~이면, 어떨까
2. 고르게, 평평하게
3. 감각
4. 잊다
5. 기억하다
6. 자연스럽게
7. 바르다, 펴다
8. 태우다
9. 서로 같은, 비슷한
10. 다른

**B**
1. date
2. similar
3. sometimes
4. future
5. during

**C**
1. outgoing
2. elementary
3. spare
4. alike
5. friendly

## Chapter 8_ Unit 20

### Check Again!

**A**
1. 불다
2. 세다, 계산하다
3. 둥근
4. 연습하다
5. 그림자
6. 성우
7. 예정, 계획
8. 전문가
9. 썩은
10. 뼈

**B**
1. flat
2. shape
3. screen
4. sharp
5. branch

**C**
1. practicing
2. created
3. schedule
4. brains
5. gate

## Chapter 8_ Unit 21

### Check Again!

**A**
1. 세기, 100년
2. 설명하다
3. 일어나다, 발생하다
4. 발명하다
5. 정기적인
6. 역사적인
7. 비행
8. 대량 생산하다
9. 의사 소통
10. 대화

**B**
1. past
2. dentist
3. pain
4. pilot
5. earlier

**C**
1. factory
2. engineer
3. invented
4. imagine
5. harmful

## Chapter 9_ Unit 22

### Check Again!

**A**
1. ~에 도착하다
2. 해안
3. 기름 유출
4. 식사
5. 정말로, 실제로
6. 깃털
7. 이웃(사람)
8. 먼
9. 용서하다
10. 씻어내다, 헹구다

**B**
1. appreciation
2. volunteer
3. seafood
4. dinner
5. pair

**C**
1. Eve
2. announced
3. shower
4. hardworking
5. village

## Chapter 9_ Unit 23

### Check Again!

**A**
1. 유인물
2. 자줏빛의
3. 표현하다
4. 염색하다
5. 허가하다, 허락하다
6. 가운데의
7. 헐렁한
8. 규칙
9. 밑줄을 긋다
10. 개성

**B**
1. unfair
2. colorful
3. boring
4. firm
5. uniform

**C**
1. regulations
2. Either
3. colorful
4. express
5. reason

## Chapter 9_ Unit 24

### Check Again!

**A**
1. 지도
2. 지식
3. 충분한
4. 사막
5. 전쟁
6. 군인
7. 상상하다
8. 메시지
9. ~사이에
10. 가사

**B**
1. weapon
2. peace
3. education
4. language
5. border

**C**
1. agreed
2. education
3. Gestures
4. difficulty
5. protect

## Chapter 10_ Unit 25

### Check Again!

**A**
1. 보기, 예
2. 국제적인, 국제간의
3. 값이 더 싼
4. 야외의
5. 시장
6. 백화점
7. 쿠폰, 할인권
8. 전기
9. 무선의
10. 플러그를 뽑다

**B**
1. save
2. chat
3. goods
4. sale
5. wise

**C**
1. night
2. shopping
3. save
4. chat
5. turn

## Chapter 10_ Unit 26

### Check Again!

**A**
1. ~할 여유가 있다
2. 비싼
3. 상, 포상
4. (경기 등에) 참가시키다
5. 사진
6. 빌다, 간청하다
7. 서다, 일어서다
8. 훌륭한
9. 성공하다
10. 쓰다, 소비하다

**B**
1. ticket
2. ad(advertisement)
3. hate
4. job
5. thirsty

**C**
1. skateboard
2. model
3. pose
4. sunglasses
5. reward

## Chapter 10_ Unit 27

### Check Again!

**A**
1. 인정이 있는, 친절한
2. 멋진, 시원한
3. 빌리다
4. 유명한
5. 되돌아오다(가다)
6. 훔치다
7. 어쨌든, 아무튼
8. 조언, 충고
9. 좋아하는
10. 용서하다

**B**
1. cute
2. brand-new
3. deep
4. leave
5. tight

**C**
1. attention
2. breath
3. advice
4. except
5. fit

## Chapter 11_ Unit 28

### Check Again!

**A**
1. 기계
2. 한 장, 시트
3. 천재
4. 가구
5. 혼합하다, 섞다
6. 운전하다
7. 구부리다
8. 초대하다
9. 자주, 종종
10. 무거운

**B**
1. compact
2. greet
3. carry
4. serve
5. clever

**C**
1. smile
2. flour
3. greet
4. downtown
5. plenty

# Chapter 11_ Unit 29

## Check Again!

**A**
1. 지난, 마지막의
2. 정보
3. 도서관
4. 사교성 있는
5. 기술
6. 현대의
7. 졸업
8. 식, 의식
9. 대여하다
10. 문명, 문화

**B**
1. take a picture
2. join
3. member
4. repair
5. matter

**C**
1. cheer
2. matter
3. belong
4. full
5. convenient

# Chapter 12_ Unit 30

## Check Again!

**A**
1. 공해, 오염
2. 세계적인, 전 세계의
3. 환경
4. 토론하다, 논의하다
5. 똑같게, 균등하게
6. 줄이다
7. 유용한
8. 텅 빈
9. 씨앗
10. 싹트다, 나기 시작하다

**B**
1. topic
2. affect
3. reuse
4. wallet
5. grow

**C**
1. jeans
2. soap
3. fashion
4. cooking
5. treat

# Chapter 12_ Unit 31

## Check Again!

**A**
1. 기사, 논설
2. 열기구 타기
3. 풍경
4. 열기구 비행사
5. (풍선 등을) 부풀게 하다
6. 활동, 운동
7. 통제하다
8. 사고
9. 예보, 예상
10. 온화한, 순한

**B**
1. mind
2. pilot
3. course
4. leisure
5. perfect

**C**
1. hot-air
2. filled
3. means
4. controlled
5. landed

# Chapter 12_ Unit 32

## Check Again!

**A**
1. 갑자기
2. 천둥
3. 이상한, 묘한
4. 곧은, 똑바로 선
5. 비밀
6. 정적인, 정전기의
7. 매체, 매개물
8. 위험한
9. 전지, 배터리
10. 만지다, 건드리다

**B**
1. leader
2. hear
3. stick
4. tool
5. scientist

**C**
1. about
2. blown
3. explained
4. active
5. experiments

Answer Key **271**

|  | 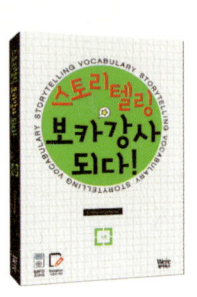 |  |  |
|---|---|---|---|
| 권 구분(Color) | **GREEN** | **BLUE** | **RED** |
| 대상 (권장) | 초급 | 중급 | 고급 |
| 어휘 수 | 약 1,300개 | 약 2,000개 | 약 2,500개 |
| 지문 | 총 32 Unit | 총 36 Unit | 총 40 Unit |
| 공통사항 | 총 12 Chapter | | |